AF505054

"**Break Free…Live Free** is a powerful battle plan to overcome strongholds and to set you on a path of freedom and healing."
—**Rebecca Nichols Alonzo,** *New York Times* best-selling author

BREAK FREE LIVE FREE

Dismantling the Strongholds that Sabotage Your Future

SARAH MACLEOD

ENDORSEMENTS

"This book has invaluable information on strongholds. What they are, how they've lied to us, and how to get rid of them. The teaching Sarah MacLeod has brought to these pages has been walked out for many years and are tried and true. Don't pass up the opportunity to dive deeper in the pool of understanding that the Lord has provided for us in His Word and in this book."
Ricky Skaggs, 15 time-Grammy-winning country, bluegrass and gospel artist

"Whether you are aware of strongholds in your life, or need help discovering them, Sarah's personal journey, along with her experience helping countless others, is conveyed in *Break Free, Live Free*. Its powerful message will guide you on your path to healing and freedom!"
Rebecca Nichols Alonzo, *New York Times* best-selling author of *The Devil in Pew Number Seven*

I have known and admired Sarah MacLeod for many years. She is a woman of strong faith and deep compassion. She is a naturally gifted communicator with the heart of a teacher. In her book *Break Free, Live Free,* Sarah teaches us that strongholds are common to people all over the world regardless of race or culture. She uncovers the lies we believe about ourselves, about others, and especially about GOD! These lies make us feel bound and isolated, and they prevent us from fulfilling our destiny and purpose. This book is filled with HOPE! I agree with Sarah that it is possible that we could see a "tidal wave of liberation" flood the world, even in our lifetime. As each one of us experiences personal freedom, we can help others do the same, and see His Kingdom come"

Sharon White-Skaggs, multiple grammy-winning, country, bluegrass, and gospel artist

"Break Free, Live Free is a beautiful read! Ideal for those on a healing journey from strongholds, MacLeod's gifting and experience guides readers to dismantle strongholds so they can enjoy the freedom the Lord wants to bring. If you want to experience true freedom in the Lord, this book is for you."

Ashley Hetherington, author of the *The Joy of the In-Between*

"Sarah is a powerful conduit of God's love and wisdom, overflowing with nurture and safety. Having journeyed from brokenness to freedom herself, she has learned God-given tools for healing and freedom, which are included in *Break Free, Live Free.* She has been instrumental in helping me unlock parts of my heart to allow God to bring deep inner healing I never knew was possible. I'm confident this book will be a beacon of hope and transformation for many."

Pattie Mallette, mother of Justin Bieber and *New York Times* best-selling author of *Nowhere But Up*

©2024, by Sarah MacLeod
Break Free…Live Free: Dismantling the Strongholds that Sabotage Your Future
Editor: Loral Pepoon
Publisher: Harvest Sound LLC
Author Headshot Photography: emilyannephotoart.com
ISBNs—paperback: 979-8-9916989-0-0; eBook: 979-8-9916989-1-7;
Hardback 979-8-9916989-2-4

Unless otherwise stated, Scripture quotations are taken from THE HOLY BIBLE, NEW INTERNATIONAL VERSION®, NIV® Copyright © 1973, 1978, 1984, 2011 by Biblica, Inc.® Used by permission. All rights reserved worldwide. Scripture quotations are taken from The ESV® Bible (The Holy Bible, English Standard Version®). ESV® Text Edition: 2016. Copyright © 2001 by Crossway, a publishing ministry of Good News Publishers. The ESV® text has been reproduced in cooperation with and by permission of Good News Publishers. Unauthorized reproduction of this publication is prohibited. All rights reserved. Scripture quotations are taken from The Holy Bible, Bearn Standard Bible, BSB is produced in cooperation with Bible Hub, Discovery Bible, OpenBible.com, and the Berean Bible Translation Committee. This text of God's Word has been dedicated to the public domain.

Notice of Rights: All rights reserved. No part of this book may be reproduced or transmitted in any form by any means, electronic, mechanical, photocopy, recording or other without the prior written permission of the author.

Permission: For information on getting permission for reprints and excerpts, contact sarahmacleodwellness@gmail.com.

Notice of Liability: The author has made every effort to check and ensure the accuracy of information presented in this book. However, the information herein is sold without warranty, either expressed or implied. Neither the author, publisher, nor any dealer or distributor of this book will be held liable for any damages caused either directly or indirectly by the instructions and information contained in this book.

Other than the author, some names have been changed to protect the privacy of individual.

Copyright: In accordance with the U.S. Copyright Act of 1976, the scanning, uploading, and electronic sharing of any part of this book without the permission of the author is unlawful piracy and theft of the author's intellectual property. If you would like to use material from this book (other than for review purposes), prior written permission must be obtained by contacting Sarah MacLeod at sarahmacleodwellness@gmail.com.

Printed in the United States of America

Disclaimer: The conversations in this book all come from the author's recollections, as well as, several of the individuals featured in this book. They are not written to represent word-for-word transcripts. Rather the author has re-told them in a way that evokes the feeling and meaning of what was said. In all instances, the essence of the dialogue is a close and accurate account of what took place. The author has changed the names of several individuals and places, and may have changed some identifying characteristics and details for the protection of many in this book.

CONTENTS

AN INVITATION TO BREAK FREE

What if you could break free from crushing thoughts that tell you that no matter what you do, you will never be good enough, smart enough, or perform well enough?

What if you understood that the forces pulling you down are felt by all people in all cultures? What if you grasped that you aren't alone in feeling discouraged or wanting to give up at times?
What if the very things the enemy sent to break you, God could use to free you?

What if you learned from someone who faced her own breaking points and later understood and broke free from these forces pulling her down? What if the person you learned from had also helped thousands of others get free—and what if she were going to share this process with you?

Would you want to accept that invitation?

Hi, I'm Sarah MacLeod, a pastor's wife who's been leading a healing ministry and church alongside my husband since 1993. But long before we started the church and for several years after that, I was suffering under the weight and the influence of oppressive strongholds—and I didn't even know it.

I was privileged to be raised in a loving family; however, it was extremely competitive when it came to education and preparing to be a professional. I pushed myself to excel in school, and after I graduated, I became successful in my medical career. Although everything looked good on the outside, I experienced several breaking points along the way that almost took me out. Here is a sample of some of the things I faced that were devastating when I experienced them, but in retrospect, they were defining moments that profoundly shaped my future.

- At four years old in the woods of India, I found myself running for my life from a king cobra snake that was coming straight toward me in all-out attack mode.

- As I grew up and became a young adult, I sat in church hearing another good sermon, suddenly gripped with the realization that there had to be much more than what I was hearing.

- I did everything possible to live up to the American dream and climb the ladder of success only to find it was empty and lonely once I got to the top.

- I had a devastating meltdown alone in my closet feeling like I couldn't go on one more day because I felt like a failure as a wife and a mother.

- I realized that the pursuit of education and knowledge was more of an endless and fleeting pursuit of ego and titles.

- I realized that my love for people was limited and stifled by status and class.

In this journey of life, you will undoubtedly experience multiple breaking points. My friends, I'm here to tell you that each experience can be used to help you understand how to break free from the forces that try to bind you and break you. I want to show you how to turn these breakdowns into breakthroughs...I want you to see how these difficulties can become a great catalyst from which you, once and for all, decide to break free and live free.

I found that my perceived roadblocks were actually blessings in disguise since they brought me to the end of myself. And that end is where freedom begins. Despite relentless resistance through the years, I concluded that it was high time for me to finally break free and get on with my destiny!

But how would I break free? That was the big question!

In this book, I will share with you the truths I learned to break free, which I have also shared with thousands of people from all walks of life. I will help you experience new freedom—a lasting freedom that not only allows you to break free but to stay free.

If you accept this invitation to break free, you will:

- Become empowered as you begin to understand that your value and worth is not based on what others say about you.
- Learn to grow from your failures without allowing them to define your identity.

- Be inspired by new ideas and dreams beyond what you could have imagined.

You are born to be free—not weighed down by dysfunctional strongholds that hold you captive and ultimately make you apathetic, rebellious, depressed, or even destructive. These strongholds are woven into the very fabric of our culture, families, and our lineage. They are not easily discerned. But once we identify them, they can be dismantled. I'll give you the lens you need to see these strongholds and the tools you need to uproot them!

To help you see how this uprooting is possible, I'll share my amazing journey and the profound discoveries that I found during my quest to get loosed from that which once held me captive!

So, I invite you to go on this journey with me. I not only want to give you keys to unlock your destiny, purpose, and future but I also want to introduce you to the ultimate Liberator himself—or to help you get to know Him better.

You might be at that place now where you are ready to break free—that's wonderful!

Or you might not know you need freedom, but you are ready to explore the marvelous possibilities of liberty.

Either way, this book will help you break free. Are you ready?

AN INTRODUCTION TO STRONGHOLDS

Before we go much further, I need to tell you more about the obstacles to freedom so that we can work toward overcoming them. As I briefly mentioned in the last section, the word that we need to understand for our journey is stronghold. The dictionary definition of a stronghold is "a fortified place."[1] It actually comes from the Greek word "ochuroma,"[2] which means fortress. A physical fortress is built so that it is impenetrable and almost impossible to tear down. Just as there are physical strongholds, there can also be spiritual and mental strongholds.

My simple working definition of a stronghold is "an accumulation of destructive lies that have become fortified in our minds." A spiritual or mental stronghold is also difficult to tear down. These strongholds start with a lie or a series of lies that are constructed and become embedded in our minds. Over time, these lies can dominate us and cause great damage. Strongholds also can be formed by life circumstances, generational lines, and cultural influences. To tear down a stronghold, it takes the truth, which I will share in this book so that we can truly break free and live free.

Strongholds are widespread in our society and are common to mankind. Anytime we are struggling, we often tend to think we are the only one wrestling with the resulting difficulty. In reality, these strongholds are imbedded in our cultures, our families, as well as our generational family lines. They can be ancient, devilish, and hard to discern.

Regardless of the damage these strongholds can bring, they are often normalized in our society. We are living in a time when many challenges are upon us, including threats of global wars, racial and economic crises, and rumors of additional pandemics. We need to be fully alert and sober, discerning truth from lies, so we ensure that we are not trapped in the deception of strongholds—not just on a personal level but on a societal level. Despite the widespread effect of strongholds, they must be exposed in our personal lives before we can remove their effects on our society.

USING THIS BOOK

In this book, we unravel five specific strongholds that are exceedingly detrimental in many of our lives no matter how you are raised or culture you are immersed in.

1. **dead religion**
2. **performance**
3. **knowledge**
4. **mammon (love of money)**
5. **prejudice**

To walk you through how each of the strongholds affect you personally as well as the culture, to give you hope with the story of how I broke through, and to provide you with tools that you can use to break free, I've broken each stronghold sections into the following subsections:

"My Story," which recounts my experience with the stronghold, how I became ensnared in it, and how it affected me.

"Finding My Freedom," which explains how I was led into lasting freedom from the stronghold.

"Exposing the Stronghold," which will help you realize how destructive the stronghold can be to a person's life and to society, so that you grasp why breaking free from the stronghold is the key to a powerful life.

"Escaping the Stronghold," which provides a picture of what breaking free will look like for those who accept the invitation from God, who provides the power and the path for every person to be set free.

"Assessing Yourself," which offers a list of identifiers to see if the stronghold has been negatively impacting your life. This section also includes reflection questions to prepare your heart for action.

"Stepping Into Your Freedom," which provides you with a clear roadmap to personal freedom from the stronghold. This is the section that I have used in our inner healing ministry (called Inside Out) with thousands of others for more than three decades with success. I have also included foundational scriptures for you to meditate on to help you replace the lies with the truth, to renew your mind, and to reset your belief system so that it is in alignment with God's Word.

As you go through each subsection, you will be able to identify the stronghold, assess if it has a hold of you, break free from it, and learn to live free.

AN INVITATION TO LIVE FREE

I'm here to tell you the good news that lasting freedom from these strongholds *is* possible! Though it has taken decades, I have experienced this freedom personally. I am convinced it can happen for you as well, and I want to share some wisdom with you that could save years of pain by equipping you with tools I wish I had. I believe the truths that I share in this book, that I have paid a dear price to uncover, will help you find a faster track to freedom! If we can identify the hidden strongholds at the root of our behaviors, we can uproot them. We can then break free from enslavement, and we can enjoy lasting freedom.

I'd like to invite you to join me on this exciting freedom journey where we will identify and dismantle strongholds to experience lasting transformation. My hope and prayer is that God will use my story, along with the wisdom that I have discovered and carefully included in this book. You might have noticed that I mentioned

God. Yes, I believe He is THE KEY to everlasting freedom! You will see how He can empower you to not only break free but to live free!

As each of us embraces this freedom, God will use our breakthroughs not only for our benefit, but also He will empower us to liberate others. I've seen this amazing ripple effect extend out from my personal breakthroughs that caused me to become a conduit of freedom to thousands of people. And I know that He wants your future freedom to greatly impact those in your sphere of influence too. All we have to do is cooperate with God and let Him rewire our minds. Then, we will have the ultimate victory over the enemy's plan to sabotage the abundant lives we were meant to live, and a tidal wave of liberation will flood the world!

So let's begin!

DEAD RELIGION

True spirituality that is pure in the eyes of our Father God is to make a difference in the lives of the orphans, and widows in their troubles, and to refuse to be corrupted by the world's values (James 1:27, TPT).

MY STORY

My life, like most everyone's, has been marked with contradictions. I've experienced tremendous blessings as well as pain and brokenness. My life started as a fairy tale in a beautiful and mysterious land, but it soon became a nightmare. Little did I know as I was growing up and experiencing early adulthood that I was becoming ensnared in strongholds—one being dead religion. Religion, like life, may encompass contradictions. Religion can be exceedingly beneficial when it's done God's way; religion, however, can also be a great source of pain and bondage when it is twisted. Some of you may also be wondering what "dead religion" is. By definition in the Greek (an original biblical language), the word "dead" is nekros. Nekros can be translated as "lifeless and powerless."3 Therefore, dead religion is religion that is lifeless and powerless.

In my story that follows, I will relay my experiences with life-giving religion as well as the effects of dead religion, which eventually turned into a stronghold. Then I can move into the glorious part—how God set me free, once and for all—from dead religion.

My Early Childhood in India

Known as home to one of the Seven Wonders of the World, the Taj Mahal, India is a land of wonder, beauty, and mystery. Majestic, snow-capped Himalayan mountains define the country's most northern border while lush jungles and vibrant blue oceans mark the southern landscapes. The air is filled with aroma of savory spices that blend to make India's finest cuisine. Scents from curry leaves, crushed cardamom, cinnamon, cumin, and coriander delight the senses just as the rich colors of saris (Indian dresses) brighten the streets. India is a vibrant, bustling, and beautiful country. With a booming population of more than 1.4 billion[4], India is the second most populous nation in the world, quickly catching up to China.

If you were to explore India, you would find some of the most kind-hearted, beautiful people in the world. They value a rare form of hospitality with multigenerational honor and love from the youngest to the oldest family members. I experienced this multigenerational society firsthand in the early years of my life. At the age of one, I was given to my widowed grandmother, who was going to raise me in India until my parents, who had received scholarships for their doctorates in the United States, finished their degrees. What Satan may have meant for harm to try to make me feel abandoned, God turned for good because I honestly thought my grandmother was sent from Heaven. She poured every minute she had into me. I, in turn, loved her like a child would love a mother. I had everything life could offer me.

Because my grandmother was wealthy, and wealthy Indian families had servants, I grew up with people who tended to me from the moment I woke up until I went to bed. These people made my bed every day, dressed me, washed all my clothes, played with me, climbed coconut trees to get me fresh coconut water and mangoes every day, and milked my goats and cows so I would have fresh milk. At the age of three, I had my own chauffeur who took me into the city. If you have seen the show Downton Abbey (about an upper-class family in England), that was my lifestyle—with an Asian twist! Perhaps my clothes were not quite as extravagant and my home was not as large as they are on the show, but you get the idea. You could say I was spoiled.

Seeds of Life-Giving Religion Planted

When I was four years old, something extraordinary happened that changed the trajectory of my life. When I thought life could not get any better, my grandmother, whom I call Ammachy, sat me down and said she had something important to tell me. Her beliefs and the news she was going to share was quite unexpected and rare for an Indian woman. Let me explain why.

India is comprised of spiritually-minded people who believe in multitudes of gods. In fact, India is the birthplace of some of the world's largest religions—Hinduism, Buddhism and Sikhism, and Jainism. With all these religions, the chances for someone like me to have NOT grown up in one of these religions would seem slim. Amazingly, because of a unique 2000-year-old true story that originated in my home state of Kerala, located in the southern portion of India, my family lineage was forever shaped and changed.

This story starts with an unlikely man who traveled to my continent from the Middle East—a Hebrew man named Thomas. Thomas was one of the original 12 disciples of Jesus Christ, who came to India for the purpose of sharing a strange and yet wondrous story. Thomas preached the good news, sharing that Jesus is the Savior, who came to deliver the people of the world from their sins and from their feeble and failing attempts to reach a perfect God in their own strength. Thomas ultimately ended up giving his life to deliver this message to the Indian people; he became a martyr in my country, perished by the spear. Therefore, this message was extremely costly. They may have killed the messenger, but they did not stop the message! Thomas' blood seemed to propel the story, which spread like wildfire. As a result of this good news about Jesus, this life-giving message has been passed down through the generations in India. Despite the prominence of other religions in the country, and the persecution of some Christians for centuries there, my grandmother came to know Jesus.

When I was four years old, Ammachy shared the story of Jesus with me. She told me that out of God's great love for humanity he sent us Jesus, His perfect Son, to rescue us from the sin that separated us from our Heavenly Father. Jesus lived a perfect sinless life here on Earth, but then He was falsely accused by the religious leaders of His day. Jesus was betrayed, beaten, and ultimately executed on a cross. There he bled and died to take away the guilt, sin, and punishment of the world. My grandmother told me that God would forgive and remove my sin and shame as well. I knew I had done wrong. Even at a young age, I was convicted of my sin. And then and there, at my grandmother's home, I received Jesus as my Lord and Savior. I was miraculously born again. I was a new creation with a new beginning. And I was overjoyed!!

Ammachy then told me what Jesus could do for my life. I will never forget her saying, "Sarah, whatever you ask when you pray to HIM, if you believe, you will receive it."

"Why would Jesus answer my prayers?" I asked.

She answered, "He loves the hearts of children because of their simple faith and trust."

As I pondered this conversation in my bed that night, I decided I did not need to pray for more material things; I was surrounded with more material blessings than I knew what to do with. I was so moved by a God who would love everyone so much that He would even die for us and even heal the sick. I decided to ask Jesus if He would restore anyone around me who was ill and needed healing. The next day, I asked Ammachy if it was okay for me to pray for someone who was suffering with an illness. She said, "of course," and she proceeded to give me the names of the servants in her household who were sick.

One by one, I prayed a simple prayer for each person, with complete trust that Jesus would heal them. Within a day or two, I was hearing about how God was healing them as I prayed. At such a young age, I realized that my God was a supernatural miracle-worker, and He loved to heal. If a four-year-old could pray and see healings happen, anyone can. God became so real to me! Even at four years old, He became my first love.

In my early childhood, with my grandmother's unconditional love and being surrounded by the bountiful beauty of our tropical plantation, everything seemed immaculate and perfect. My life felt much like the first story in the Bible with Adam and Eve, the first humans, who were created by God and put in a perfect garden with everything they ever needed.

Everything Changed with an Unbelievable Event

I can remember the day that my enchanted life began to change. If Jesus had not made Himself so real to me and demonstrated His love for me prior to this time period that started on that fateful day, there is no way I would have been able to endure all that was ahead of me.

I was out gathering sticks for my grandmother's wood stove, and while I was in the field, I looked up and saw a massive king cobra slithering toward me in an aggressive manner. It was in all-out attack mode—its head was raised high off the ground. Terrified, all I could think of was to drop the sticks and run for my life as fast as I could. I knew that I was in grave danger, and death was closing in. In a cold sweat, I bolted through the marshes and rice paddy fields, not looking back. I had so much adrenaline going through me! I made it to my grandmother's house, absolutely out of breath with my heart pounding out of my chest, and I slammed the kitchen door behind me. As I turned around, I realized I had somehow outrun the serpent, which in reality, is almost impossible especially for a little child.

Many years later, I began to wonder: *So, what was that attempted snake attack all about? Why would a king cobra chase me?* As many know, in the Bible the snake who appears in the garden of Eden with Adam and Eve represents Satan. The enemy used temptation to deceive and enslave the first two humans. And starting with the point that Eve chose to believe Satan over what God had said, everything began to fall apart. The entrance of sin and darkness ultimately caused a terrible separation from God. Death and estrangement began to spread like a cancerous and fatal disease for people throughout time.

I believe that the cobra I saw in India was sent by the ancient snake himself: Satan, the adversary of mankind. He is described as a thief that comes to steal kill and destroy as it says in John 10:10. He had the same purpose in my life—to destroy it—just like he did in the beginning of creation with Adam and Eve. In their lives, and mine, and in everyone's lives in between, Satan's ultimate goal has been to dismantle oneness and trust between God and His children. Satan was trying to rob me of the life-giving religion I had living with my grandmother.

Soon after the snake incident, my parents came back from the U.S. to visit me in India. They realized that I was living a spoiled, undisciplined life. They began working on a visa so that I could join them in the U.S., but that would take some time. In the meantime, they moved me away from my grandmother to live with family friends in a faraway city. My parents thought these friends would discipline me more than my grandmother had.

As you can imagine, I was heartbroken to leave my grandmother and my charmed life. One year after I relocated, I had a mental breakdown. After the move, I cried myself to sleep every night waiting for my grandmother to rescue me. I found out that the cry of my heart was being heard as my parents' friends told my grandmother how distressed I was. My grandmother sent a private car to pick me up and bring me back to her. Just before the car arrived, my parents' friends received a call from my parents with a message to tell the driver to not pick me up to take me back to my grandmother's house. I know my parents thought me staying at their friends' house was for my own good, but this five-year-old was devastated. I endured another 12 months with my parents' friends until I finally was issued a visa from the consulate of India to travel to the US to meet and live with my parents. Two years after the king cobra encounter when I was six years old, I moved to America.

My Experience with Religion Growing Up in the U.S.

From the age of six to 23, after I had moved to America, I went to a Lutheran, Methodist, Presbyterian, and finally a Baptist church. By age 19, I was leading women's Bible studies in my university because I loved understanding God's Word and sharing it with my friends. We studied the Word together, and my prayer life was strong. What was missing for me was a lack of sensitivity or compassion for the broken or poor. I didn't think about them because I was in circles of people who were middle class Americans and didn't tend to interact with people different from themselves. Also, I was usually just with my family and friends most of the time, so I wasn't in areas where I even came across people in poverty. By age 22, through the spiritual disciplines of praying, reading the Bible and memorizing it, teaching the Bible in Bible studies, and living basic 10 commandments, I had established a friendship with God. In the middle of a message from the minister at my Baptist Church, when I was 23, I was thinking to myself, *There has to be more than what the pastor is telling me about God.* Something was missing or not complete. I had never forgotten the miraculous healings I had experienced in India. I wondered why I had not seen or heard teaching for all these years on people in the church getting freed from addictions or experiencing healing power as people of God prayed and laid hands on the sick.

I continued to go through the motions of attending church, singing hymns, and listening to great teachings from this pastor, but I was still feeling not fully alive in my faith. I began to wonder, *Am I following a religion that talks about Jesus but not living out of relationship in Jesus that leads to an abundant, transformed life? Why was the power of God not being demonstrated in church?* I was feeling dead inside, but I knew I wanted to be fully alive in Christ because He promised to give me life and that I would have it abundantly (John 10:10). I was also concerned about the powerless religion because of the scripture, "having a form of godliness but denying it's power." (2 Timothy 3:5, ESV). I didn't want to have a "form" of godliness. I wanted to have a vibrant experience with God that I had tasted as a four-year-old in India.

Even though I loved Jesus and had faith for mountains to be moved and for the sick healed of infirmities and diseases, I had approached religion based on the mentality that doing "good works" and following the commandments was going to get me into Heaven. Even though I was a Christian, looking back, I realized I had a wrong impression of good works because I had been unknowingly influenced by Indian culture, which is shaped by Hinduism and its works. I'll share more of that part of the story in the upcoming section called "Exposing the Strongholds." For now, suffice it to say that I believed the more I did for God, the more He would love and reward me. The more I went to church, the more Bible studies I led, the more scriptures I memorized, the more leadership positions I took at church, the more hours I prayed, the more I believed God would approve of my life and bless me. All this activity, and yet, I was left feeling exhausted trying to please God but never measuring up. This works-based mindset left me empty and lifeless inside. I felt dead spiritually.

FINDING MY FREEDOM

In my 20s in my Baptist church, I began searching my heart about what was missing in my spiritual life. The Lord answered in a surprising way. One day, a handsome, six-foot tall man came waltzing into my young adult professional class at church. I ended up marrying that man, and our love story is quite unbelievable!

Before I met my husband, Scott, I was one week away from my family securing an arranged marriage to an Indian man. These plans were interrupted by God, who showed me very clear signs that *He* wanted to arrange my marriage.

This man, Scott, who I met in class at church had something special—something intriguing. His eyes sparkled with a light when he talked about God. I had never seen that in any human before. The deep, contagious love that he had for God and Jesus was remarkable. It made me quite jealous and curious about how this man's heart was so full of love and joy. I had felt joy somewhat like his in my relationship with Jesus when it began in India thanks to my godly grandmother, but this man somehow had even more joy than I remembered. I wanted that "more." When I attended his church and experienced the worship with music, I felt like I was floating. All of a sudden, I started to cry. I felt something that I had never felt in church before. I began to feel overwhelmed with God's presence all around me; I could tell that He was so close to me in this place. All I could do was weep. During that first church service when I wept, which was before my husband and I were married, I did not fully understand what had happened. However, I do know, looking back, that being in the presence of God at that service was Him beginning to set me free from the stronghold of dead religion. Something was rekindled that reminded me of the child-like faith I had as a four-year-old in India.

I had an even deeper faith-building experience when I discovered the Holy Spirit in 1994, less than a year after Scott and I married. In Christianity, God, Jesus, and the Holy Spirit are One; they are called the Trinity. The Holy Spirit is the part of God given to believers after Jesus ascended to Heaven. None of the denominations I had been in spoke of the Baptism of the Holy Spirit. When I had been married about a year, one of our friends came over and prayed for me. In my living room, this friend prayed for the Holy Spirit to fill me, and that is what happened. Wow! I felt a rush of power flowing over me from head to toe and warmth moving through me and filling me. In this deep place, I felt God touching me, and it was the first time in my entire life when I actually felt the living God inside my body.

What I experienced is called the Baptism of the Holy Spirit. This immersion of the Holy Spirit supernaturally activates gifts and the power of God descends upon us when we invite the Holy Spirit to fill us. Acts 1:5 states, "For John baptized with water, but…you will be baptized with the Holy Spirit." On that day, I received many spiritual gifts that I am still using today. I also believe that this experience—receiving the Baptism of the Holy Spirit—was a key step for me in finding freedom from the stronghold of dead religion. (To learn more about the gifts that come with the Baptism of the Holy Spirit, read 1 Corinthians 12:4, 6–11.)

Another part of my breakthrough from dead religion started right after we were married in 1993, when I followed my husband into an unusual mission field. No, our mission field was not Africa or India; it was in my own city of Nashville, Tennessee, in the United States. This part of Nashville is known as the inner city or the "hood," and at the time, it was filled with extreme poverty. I was surprised to learn that large cities in an advanced nation like the

United States of America could have such brokenness and devastation. I learned that inner cities were largely ignored and basically left to self-destruct.

I lived in the suburbs and was blind to what was going on in these areas. My suburban environment had been one of barre classes and children's soccer games, lattes, and SUVs. The inner-city communities in desperate need were out of sight, out of mind. I did not understand the depth of what my husband felt called to do. After we married, he felt compelled to lay down his successful music career and serve the underserved. At the time, I was climbing the ladder of success in my physical therapy career, and this turn of events did not make sense. This calling was not congruent with what I imagined for our lives, nor did it fit the mold of what my Asian Indian culture had instilled in me. The lifestyle we would have to live to accept this calling was not in line with the rest of American society, and I had no framework for it from my churches or family.

Prior to our marriage, my fiancé had already been working with the homeless in downtown Nashville. I remember one day after church he took me to eat pizza. He had invited some of his homeless friends to eat with us. After the meal, we walked outside to go to our car, and two of the guys that we had just eaten with broke out in a fistfight, which turned into a knife fight! I was scared for my life, but I was also terrified that my fiancé would get hurt in the brawl when he stepped in to stop the fight. Therefore, in my mind, when he told me about what he felt called to do, I was not sure about taking care of the poor and homeless if it meant endangering our lives. At the time when this fight took place, I was grateful that my fiancé did not do this ministry full-time.

However, our situation changed soon after we got married because that's when my husband felt compelled to serve the poor full time. I was not going to fight him on it because I could see such passion and excitement and life coming from his heart. One of the reasons I married him was that I saw his heart of justice, which had become even more determined to help broken people.

With the help of some friends, Scott started serving the heart of one of the roughest inner-city communities in Nashville. Back then, in the 1990s, this area of town was called John Henry Hale housing projects, nicknamed "Jo Johnston" because of the name of the main street that runs through the area. This community was decaying with addictions, hopelessness, isolation, and pain tucked away in the heart of the city. Day and night, the community was overtaken with drug deals, murders, gang fights, cruel dog fights, and prostitution.

For decades, there was so much devastation in this area that I was wondering if doing our part was even going to make a difference in changing the lives of those who lived in Jo Johnston. I understood why few people would go anywhere near that place unless they were undercover cops. In fact, that's precisely who many residents thought my husband was! But he had a different purpose. He wanted to serve and love them. He had been undone while reading the red letters, the words of Jesus. He was particularly moved by Matthew 25:31–46, a passage in which Jesus says that if you fed or clothed the least of these, you have done it unto Me.

Although my husband wanted to stay and love people in Jo Johnston, part of me wanted to run, as I was scared out of my mind. This community seemed like the last place on earth a naïve Asian Indian like me should be. Additionally, the media made the inner city seem like a frightening place. I had been taught within my Asian Indian culture that I needed to pursue security for my future and a high paying job. I was not ready to lay my life down to serve the poor in my first-year marriage. I mean, who becomes a missionary in their own city?

I did not realize how much selfishness and self-preservation was in my heart. Fear of the unknown and fear of losing my life held me back. After a year of crying out to God for my fear to go away, I finally came to a place of surrender to His perfect love. On that day, I said to the Father, "My life is not my own—it is yours," and my fear subsided. Since then, I have learned that fear is a paralyzer, and it makes people unable to think clearly. Once I surrendered, I finally started to get a clear vision for our inner-city community. This prayer of surrender was another step in finding my freedom from the stronghold of dead religion.

As we served in this part of the city, we also had to block out the media's negative narrative that fed the fear and the division by portraying our predominately African American community as nothing but dangerous. Instead, we listened to the heart of Jesus Christ. We chose to follow His heart and His Word, and we discovered so many hidden treasures in this community. During this time, The Lord gave me a specific scripture, which says: "Speak up for those who cannot speak for themselves, for the rights of all who are destitute. Speak up and judge fairly; defend the rights of the poor and needy" (Proverbs 31:8–9).

By God's grace and with help from thousands of volunteers from all walks of life, cultures, and nationalities, we joined together and helped invest in the lives of many people—most of whom were single mothers and their children. With God's love and compassion working in and through us we had the privilege of helping change one life at a time.

The bible clearly defines pure religion in James 1:27 looking after widows, orphans, and keeping oneself from being polluted from the world. When I started serving the poor, the orphaned, and widows, I did it out of obedience. I was following what I had learned was a command, but I was not explicitly paying attention to the words of the verse. But as the years went by doing these basics, I was experiencing life like I never had in the many years I had been pursuing God. I began to see for myself that it is better to give than to receive. I started to think about the widows and orphans more than taking care of myself or my family. I began to share God's love with people who are broken and hurting, and I found joy and a more beautiful life in the process. The Lord was purifying me by removing my pride and self-serving mindset. In the process, I was starving the stronghold of dead religion, increasing my freedom. I began to live out the following verse, "Do nothing out of selfish ambition or empty pride, but in humility consider others more important than yourselves. Each of you should look not only to your own interests, but also to the interests of others" (Philippians 2:3, Berean Standard Bible).

Over time, I saw profound transformation come to multitudes of fatherless children, single mothers, and at-risk teens with love and compassion in action. I saw firsthand that love is an action word, and I began to understand and live out the principle that love without action is just a good intention. The Apostle John says: "Let us not love with words or speech but with actions and in truth" (1 John 3:18). This transformation of these people did not come with one random act of kindness but with thousands of selfless actions. Every Thursday evening, we would serve a hot, delicious meal, and we would teach people how to read the Bible. We also loved on the children every Saturday morning, when they were taught how to love themselves, their siblings, and their families. We also provided practical needs for the mothers like baby formula, diapers, and furniture. It was so rewarding to see my religion come alive again after I found freedom from the stronghold of dead religion and other strongholds. My freedom not only set me free, but it helped equip me to pour into a large community and to help set them free! I'll share more of that story in the subsequent chapters.

A Summary of My Path to Freedom

In case it's helpful, here is a summary of my steps to freedom.

My Christian faith originated because Jesus' disciple Thomas was willing to die for his faith in India—in other words, my faith is a direct result of the brave action of another. The next step was also the result of an action on the part of another person—a family member sharing her faith with me. After that, the next steps were based on my actions.

1. I accepted Jesus Christ as my Lord and Savior at four years old after my grandmother told me about Him.

2. At the age of 12, I got water baptized. Although I didn't mention it in my story, it is an important part of a journey to freedom in Christ because it symbolizes the washing away of our sin.

3. In my early 20s, I began wanting to experience more of God than I had experienced in the churches I had attended since I moved to the U.S. I was also influenced by the joy and peace I witnessed in my future husband's life. I wanted what he had! We never know how our lives in freedom will influence another!

4. After knowing Jesus for more than 20 years, at the age of 25, I discovered and experienced the power and the Baptism of the Holy Spirit, which activated new gifts of God in my life.

(To learn more about the gifts that come with the Baptism of the Holy Spirit, read 1 Corinthians 12:4, 6–11.)

5. With the power of the Holy Spirit, I was able to put my faith into action by partnering with my husband. I began sharing my faith with those who are broken and poor—people who could never give back to me. I was compelled to share because I had received God's love, and I had a vibrant relationship with him. My pure religion was not based on the work I did for God. Purity in religion was an overflow of the understanding I received from God that love is an action word.

6. I didn't describe this last step specifically in my story, but eventually I was able to help start a wholistic healing ministry that enables others to experience God's love so that they too can break free. I love healing the brokenhearted with tools God has given me to bind up their pain. As they experience the love of God through us, many of them begin to love Jesus too—and to help others. The tools I use are included in the section called "Steps to Freedom in Your Life."

EXPOSING THE STRONGHOLD

This section will help you see the potential trap of the dead religion stronghold, both for yourself and for society at large.

As a pastor's wife since 1993, I interact with many people who do not initially think this trap of "dead religion" has ensnared them. But, as I ask them a few questions, I soon discover that many are in fact gripped by this deceptive stronghold—just as I was. Here are some of the questions I have asked. I invite you to ask them of yourself.

- Do you feel like no matter what you do to try to be "good enough," you always miss the mark?

- Do you have a tradition or heritage of faith, but do you just tend to "go through the motions"?

- Do you believe in God, but He feels distant and impersonal to you?

- Do you feel God is angry and ready to punish you if you don't live up to His standards?

- Have you dabbled in or been exposed to Eastern religions? Are you drawn to horoscopes, palm readers, getting your fortune read, spells, or "good" witches?

If you answered "yes" to any of these questions, some of your life struggles may be rooted in this dangerous, devious stronghold of dead religion. No matter which of the ways you could have unknowingly come into agreement with the stronghold of dead religion, it will undoubtedly keep you spiritually and emotionally bound. If you feel confused and exhausted from the endless quest of chasing answers from a multitude of sources to find some meaning in life, you are likely under a stronghold of dead religion. The exhaustion can also come from the desire to tirelessly do things to please God. No matter what you do, it feels like it is never enough. What follows is another quick litmus test to see if your religion is leading you to a path of life or a path of death:

- Are you following a behavior because of tradition or because of something you were taught?
- Do you have compassion for the weak? If not, you may be under a stronghold of dead religion.

If you answered yes to any of these questions, you may be in bondage to this stronghold. You will have a chance to more fully assess your life and to use the tools the Lord gave me to secure your freedom at the end of this chapter. First, however, I want to relay how widespread and devastating the effects of this stronghold are. I've found this information helps people realize that they are not alone—and you aren't either!

God is powerful enough to bring massive freedom worldwide—even though the decision to embrace this freedom is one each of us needs to make. If we all do our part to dismantle this stronghold, the entire world could change!

The core problem of those who are affected by dead religion is that although these people know about God, they do not have a relationship, in other words, a friendship with, their Creator, who meticulously designed every hair on their heads. This Creator, the One True God of the Bible, made the Earth, oceans, mountains, every living creature, as well as each person who makes up the human race. If people are in a dead religion stronghold, they are likely not connected to God Almighty, the true power source. Therefore, they can't access His supernatural power.

This stronghold is more widespread than you might think. The enemy loves to make us think that we are the only one with an issue so that we isolate and don't get help. You have already read about my personal struggle. Next, I will discuss how a stronghold of dead religion affects cultures with which I'm somewhat familiar: India, the U.S., and in church leadership.

The Impact of Dead Religion in India

Part of the reason I was impacted by the stronghold of dead religion were the roots of the religions and the beliefs in the culture associate with those religions in my home country of India. In my 20s, I came to understand that even though I was born in a country that seemed to have so much faith and conviction, it was missing some basic principles of love, mercy, forgiveness, taking care of the poor, weak, and unfortunate. I also realized I had unknowingly taken on some of the harsh mentality of the Indian Hindu culture, which fosters the belief that the poor deserve being poor and oppressed. Even though I had grown up as a Christian, the beliefs of Hinduism have permeated the mindsets of most people in India, no matter what the religion they practice. The society and culture that is influenced by Hinduism is based on social classes called the caste system, which categorizes the value of people by a perceived belief of their "goodness" during a past life (reincarnation). Hindus worship multiple gods each day, and the religion has trapped millions of people into looking to these gods to reward them based on their good works and putting the destiny of their eternal lives into the hand of these gods.

It deeply saddens me in a country with a religion that worships thousands of gods, people, from my observation, seem to ignore kindness, justice, and mercy toward others. Another tenet of Hinduism, based on the caste system, is that if people are perceived to have extensive sins in their past lives, they are considered "untouchable." More than 160 million people are considered untouchable. These people are impoverished, hurting, and in pain, and yet, others leave them to suffer because the Hindu religion fosters the belief that they deserve these conditions because of their past sins. This belief gives religion the power to keep the poor trapped because traditionally they can only do menial and dirty work. Treating people this way deeply saddens me, and I feel this behavior is influenced by a demonic kingdom of darkness. A clear indicator that the stronghold of dead religion is at work is when religion is used as a justification to treat the poor in a derogatory, controlling, or destructive manner resulting in the poor becoming slaves to the rich. If you are born into the highest caste in the Hindu religion, you have all of the greatest privileges, attend the best universities, eat the most extravagant food, and live in lavish palaces. If, however, you are born into poverty, it is your destiny and lot in life to stay in poverty and shame. For all these reasons, I would say that a stronghold of dead religion has its grip in the culture in India.

The Impact of Dead Religion in American Churches

In my 20s in America, when I saw the poor in the inner cities (government-designated areas where the poor live), I believed if they worked hard and got a good education, then they could get a job, and they would not be poor. This mindset was also prevalent among my American friends and families who lived in the suburbs. Religion that is uncompassionate or does not advocate or speak up for those that are suffering in poverty is lifeless or dead. This dead religion was at work in myself as well as in many who live in the U.S.

I think multitudes of people are being lulled to sleep spiritually by dead religion in the U.S. Numerous people may still attend church out of duty, but they are not walking in the power to change their own lives, much less to make change in society. Others may only attend church because of religious tradition the way their families have attended church for generations.

Research shows that people are, in fact, already leaving churches—especially in early adulthood. According to the Barna group, the percentage of people who are 18 to 29 years old who grew up in church and are no longer active is 64%.[5] This number will only continue to increase unless this stronghold of dead religion is exposed as we start identifying its traits in our individual lives.

I believe this percentage (64%) of young adults leaving the church is so high because many in this group aren't getting what they long to see in church. They want to see that the God that they worship moves in power, and they want their religion to take care of the poor and broken. They are wanting pure, life-giving religion that is making a difference in the world around them—not just inside the church. When religion is only rooted in tradition, and when the people don't feel alive as they worship, they may have the stronghold of dead religion operating in their lives. Just as pure true religion brings people closer to God, dead religion separates people from God, which means those with dead religion may eventually leave church, abandon a moral code, and make up their own rules.

The Impact of Dead Religion on Society At Large

Some secularists might say a godless society is a good thing, but I would propose that a godless society is a society on its way to extinction. In a godless society, there is no moral compass, and each person becomes his or her own god. A godless society means no absolute truth because truth is defined by the individual's truth, which is actually feelings. As people interact without absolute truth, they may ignore or exploit the weakest and vulnerable in society such as children, elderly, widows, and orphans instead of helping them.

Sadly, dead or false religion has even been used throughout history to not only manipulate and control, but even start and justify entire wars. If we don't break free from the stronghold of dead religion, we will be in great danger of continuing to damage or even destroying our society. We will discuss more about the potential harm we face as humans as we examine additional strongholds in future chapters. For now, let's look at one last, perhaps surprising, impact of the stronghold of dead religion.

The Trap of Dead Religion for Religious Leaders

Dead religion as a stronghold doesn't just affect those who are disheartened by the church, as I was, nor does it just cause some to not care for the poor, as was the case for me. Dead religion can also be a trap for religious leaders. The trap in this context is something that Jesus explicitly warns us about in the Bible. He warns us to watch out for the teachers of the law and the Pharisees, who loved the praises of people more than the praises of God. Everything they did was to be seen by men. They were driven by a lust for power and money and position. Jesus said in Matthew 23:23–26 that outwardly these people looked virtuous and pompous for they certainly knew how to put on a big religious show. But inwardly they were "full of greed and selfish indulgence" (Matthew 23:27). Jesus confronted these religious leaders and called them whitewashed tombs. This harsh indictment means exactly what the verse says: the tombs covered with white paint looked beautiful on outside, but on the inside, they were full of the bones of the dead and everything unclean. This deadness speaks of their spiritual condition. They projected an outward image of holiness and religiosity, but inwardly, they were spiritually *dead.* They may have been ceremonially clean but inside they were despicably unclean—and full of death.

Remember the story about when I was being chased by a snake and how God showed me that was Satan himself? Jesus took this snake analogy another step further and exposed a particular stronghold that it is connected with. He explicitly compares snakes to the "religious" leaders of his day.

""You snakes! You brood of vipers! How will you escape being condemned to hell?" (Matthew 23:33).

Jesus identifies the wicked religious spirit as the serpentine force that was driving and manipulating the Pharisees and the teachers of the law. Jesus goes even further in the verses we just read, saying that these people were on a crash course toward hell if they remained under its influence. Just as Jesus warned: Dead religion is nothing to play with…it is, in fact, deadly. All people, regardless of how they see dead religion, need to identify it for what it really is—a lifeless stronghold— that leads nowhere but a dead end.

ESCAPING THE STRONGHOLD

This section is your invitation to break free so you can live free.

In this chapter, we will look at powerful passages of scripture that dismantle not only this stronghold, but all strongholds. For additional scriptures, and to learn how to apply this power to your life, please see the section: "Steps to Freedom in Your Life."

Whether we are bound in a counterfeit, works-based religion, worn-out serving God with "works" as a Christian leader, or if we are stuck in a lifeless, pagan religion like witchcraft, there is a way to begin to break free and live free from the stronghold of dead religion.

That one way to begin to break free is what I learned when I was four, through my grandmother and through the truth of God's Living Word, the Bible. The one way to ensure salvation—is through Jesus. He is the way, the truth, and the life, and no one comes to the Father except through the Son (see John 14:6). His sacrifice is the only atonement for our sin. Accepting Jesus is the first step to breaking the stronghold of dead religion—or any stronghold.

We have seen just a couple examples in this book, but we know that there are multitudes of "dead," religious theological positions floating around that are a product of dead religion. Most of them are dead because they are devoid of an intimate relationship with our Creator. Most of these ideologies rely on the works of men rather than the works of God to ensure salvation. Jesus said on the cross, "It is finished" (John 19:30). It was a finished work of giving His life that redeems us. He defeated sin and death. And because He lives, we live! Eternal life is a free gift of God offered through Jesus!

We tend to think that we have to work for His approval. But in reality, there is no one good enough to earn His complete approval. That's why the Bible tells us that "all have sinned and fallen short of the glory of God" (Romans 3:23). In other words, we *all* need a Savior! We all need to accept Jesus. Also, as I have said, He gives us a gift we cannot earn—we simply receive His gift!

The one true living God is the maker of Heaven and Earth. He doesn't just call us into a relationship, He calls us into a love relationship. The number one commandment in the Bible is to love the Lord your God with all your heart and soul and mind and strength (a paraphrase of Mark 12:30, NLT). Love is the most powerful force in the universe. The Bible tells us "God is love." And it says that "there's no greater expression of love then to lay down one's life for one's friend." And that's exactly what Jesus did for us…He became a ransom for us all who were trapped by sin and death. Jesus said that the second great commandment that was equal to the first is to "love your neighbor as you love yourself" (Mark 12:31). We are to treat others as we want to be treated (a paraphrase of Matthew 7:12). This is God's golden rule!

We are also in a time of not only being prey to strongholds, but we are subjected to great deception because of so many voices and agendas. But Jesus said you will know people by their fruit. A good tree bears good fruit, and the bad tree bears bad fruit. But how do we test the difference between good and bad or truth and a lie? God's Word, the Bible, is truth. Jesus said we can "know the truth, and the truth will set us free" (John 8:32). Without knowing the truth, without knowing God's ways that are spelled out in his Word, there's no way to accurately discern what is a lie.

I highly encourage you to fall in love with the Bible because according to Psalm 119:105, it is a lamp to our feet. I have discovered this concept time and time again. The Bible is a roadmap for life…it is where we find our moral compass and our values. Many have shared an acronym for Bible…**B**asic **I**nstructions **B**efore **L**eaving **E**arth.

After we have a loving relationship with Jesus, and we are accustomed to spending time in His Word, He then invites us to be filled and baptized by His Holy Spirit. We learn that in Luke 3:16 that Jesus will baptize us with the Holy Spirit and with fire. Jesus then says: "But very truly I tell you, it is for your good that I am going away. Unless I go away, the advocate will not come to you; but if I go, I will send him to you" (John 16:7). When we invite Jesus to baptize us with Holy Spirit, He dwells within us. He will work through us and be with us through our ups and downs or highs and lows of life.

God wants us to have the fire and power of the Holy Spirit living within us. This fire will empower us to love the world, which is broken and filled with many temptations and enticements. If we have pure, life-filled religion, we represent Him well, and we will be a vehicle that draws others to Jesus by our love.

God not only designed us for enjoyment to have a relationship with us, but also, He created us to administer justice and mercy here on Earth so that the world would be flooded with love, peace, and goodwill. In a world overflowing with these qualities, the poor would be taken care of by people who have compassion and kindness. In a world of mercy, people would not only be looking out for their own interests but also for the interests of others. Only an authentic relationship with Father God is sustainable and powerful enough to give us a long-term desire to take care of others.

What if all people on Earth snapped out of the grip of this dead religion and embraced the authentic pure, life-filled religion? I think the human soul craves the pure substance—not the polluted mixture.

Just as God's Living Water is pure, life-filled, pure religion cleanses our hearts from the destructive mixture that dead religion brings.

Because of my experience in inner city Nashville, where I and others who were steeped in dead religion are now living free, I can already envision multitudes letting go of this lifeless religion that infiltrates our society and discovering pure, life-filled religion, administering justice, mercy, and compassion. I can envision people breaking free and living free!

If you are ready to be part of this hope, and something has stirred within you, I highly encourage you to complete the next two sections.

ASSESSING YOURSELF

The Identifiers of Dead Religion

You've read about the devastating impact of dead religion. But, how, specifically, do you know if you are living under a stronghold of dead religion?

Below are 20 identifiers of the stronghold of dead religion. As you read them, put a check mark by the ones you feel apply to you. Each check mark will be considered one point. Add up the check marks, which will give you the total points for this stronghold. By the end of this book, the number of points for each stronghold will help you determine which stronghold needs the most attention. (Most people have some of each; if this happens to you, don't be discouraged. God will enable you to break free of every stronghold—it just may take some time.)

1. I tend to try to earn right standing with God by being good and keeping the rules.
2. I tend to keep records of wrongs.
3. I tend to struggle with trusting God and yielding control over to Him.
4. I tend to overlook the good qualities in other people.
5. I tend to feel afraid of God.
6. I tend to criticize and judge others.
7. I tend to feel that I need to wear a mask or lie about my struggles.
8. I tend to profess Jesus Christ as Lord, but not to trust Him.
9. I tend to continue to sin because I do not understand grace.

10. I tend to ignore the commands of Jesus (found in Matthew 10:8) to heal the sick, cleanse the unclean, raise the dead, and preach the gospel to the poor.

11. I tend to fear losing my salvation, feeling like my works earn me right standing with God and other people.

12. I do not think it is necessary to have a relationship with Jesus.

13. I tend to neglect to defend or speak up for the rights of the weak or oppressed, including children, widows, the homeless, and the most vulnerable in society.

14. I tend to exhibit apathy serving others.

15. I tend to lack compassion for the brokenhearted, imprisoned, and impoverished.

16. I tend to attend church or believe in religion because of obligation or family.

17. I believe that healing the sick was only for Jesus and his disciples to do; it's not my obligation.

18. I don't believe I have a responsibility to share my faith with others as religion is a personal decision.

19. I believe that there are many paths to God.

20. I don't believe it's necessary for me to walk in the miraculous or supernatural, as I don't want to draw any attention to myself.

Reflection Questions

Take a few moments to get quiet and think about the following reflection questions and write your answers in a journal.

1. Have you personally encountered dead religion in your life? How did it negatively affect you?
2. What symptoms of dead religion have you noticed in your life?
3. Does any part of my story relate to your life?
4. On a scale of 0–10, How would you rate the depth of care you have for the weakest and poorest in society?
5. What are two action steps you can put in place to activate pure religion?

(For example, serve your community and pray for the sick.)

If you are ready to break free from dead religion, and if you want a thriving relationship with the living God, I invite you to pray through the steps in the next section.

STEPPING INTO YOUR FREEDOM

If you recognize that the stronghold of dead religion is affecting you, then there are clear steps you can take to break free. The following steps, which encompass a biblical process of repentance and replacing lies with the truth of God's Word, are the ones I used in my personal journey of freedom. I have also used these steps for more than 30 years with thousands of others.

Repent

The first step is to repent. To repent is to turn completely in the opposite direction of the sin or mindset. In other words, it means not only to be sorry but also to take actions to go the other way. We must review our actions and acknowledge that we have allowed this stronghold to operate in our lives. We recognize that a behavior is wrong and then make a commitment to turn away from it.

Pray with me:

"God, I'm so sorry. As Your child, I repent for every way I partnered with dead religion and allowed the stronghold to rule my life, decisions, and thinking patterns. Please forgive me. Your Word says to take every thought captive to the obedience of Christ, and I am taking this captive! The stronghold of dead religion is no longer allowed to ensnare me. The beliefs that have held the stronghold of dead religion captive in my mind are being uprooted and expelled."

Renounce

To renounce a stronghold is to break agreement with toxic beliefs that have formed a stronghold. When we renounce something, we make a declaration that we no longer affiliate with that system of beliefs.

Break agreements with the following statements that apply to you. I break agreement with the stronghold of dead religion because:

- *I thought I had to earn right standing with God by being good and keeping rules.*
- *I have criticized and judged others for not following rules.*
- *I have hidden struggles and I have worn a mask so that others don't know what's really going on with me.*
- *I have ignored Jesus' commands to heal the sick, cleanse the lepers, raise the dead, and preach the gospel to those who don't yet know Him.*
- *I have lived in fear of losing salvation.*
- *I have thought that religion is an obligation.*
- *I have used wise and persuasive words but I have lacked demonstration of God's power in my life.*
- *I have thought that it's not necessary to live a pure life.*
- *I have believed that it's not necessary for me to take care of the poor.*

Declare with me:

"I renounce and break all agreements I have made with the stronghold of dead religion. Specifically, I renounce the beliefs of dead religion found in the statements above that I have just broken agreement with. I am so sorry, God, for coming into agreement with

dead religion and for how I have lived my life based on the effects of this stronghold. Please forgive me, Father God. Thank you, Father, that You are faithful to forgive me."

Release

To release is to break free. Releasing helps you let go. Make the decision not to hold onto the stronghold. Sometimes when we have a belief for so long, it can feel scary letting it go because it's so familiar. When we let the stronghold go, we are giving it to God. We allow the powerful blood of Jesus to break us free from the effects of the stronghold of dead religion. His blood washes away our sins, iniquities, or pain.

Pray with me:

"Father God, I release this stronghold of dead religion and place it at Your feet. Break me free from all the ways the stronghold of dead religion has affected my life and those around me. Today I choose to fully receive You and live my life with the values of pure, life-filled religion. I choose to fully love You with all my heart. Remove me from the grip of the stronghold and release me from its affects. Jesus, I plead Your blood over my life and the stronghold of dead religion. I receive the power of Your blood to wash and renew me."

Restore

To restore is to bring something back to its original condition. When God restores us, we are even better than we were before. Everything that the enemy has stolen from your life, I believe God wants to restore to you a hundredfold.

Can you imagine being 100 times better than how you were? 100 times more potent? 100 times more fruitful? So, ask God what

He wants to restore to you or to give to you as you let go of dead religion. In my life, He has given me a vibrant relationship in which I'm excited to spend time in the Word—not out of obligation or duty—but because I just want to spend time with God…He is my best friend. The "rhythms" He has given me enable me to live out pure religion.

These rhythms include waking up every day and acknowledging the Holy Spirit. I ask Him to empower me as I tune into His voice. I take about five minutes to listen to worship music to get in His presence, and I quiet my soul. I usually take three deep breaths, thank Him for my day, and ask Him to direct my steps. I then take at least five minutes every morning reading the Bible. I ask Jesus to help me live out what I read if there is a command in the verse. For example, if I read a verse that says to give to people in need or feed the hungry, I ask Him for a way to carry out that instruction.

Now, it's your turn. I encourage you to ask God what He wants to restore in your life in place of dead religion. Perhaps this restoration will include a more vibrant, active relationship with Him so that you can live in freedom—a marker of life-giving religion.

Pray with me:

"God, what do You want to restore to me in place of dead religion?"

God may say something specific to you in response to this prayer. If He does, I encourage you to record His answer and to praise Him for it! Then, to help seal His work, move on to the next step.

Rewire

To rewire your thinking patterns is to think only the thoughts God thinks about you. This shift is restructuring your thinking, which comes out of what you believe about yourself and the world around you. We are replacing old, dysfunctional thought patterns with new, healthy ones. To rewire, we create "I am" statements. These statements are built on the truth of who you are, according to God's Word. I encourage you to read these truths over yourself for at least the next 60 days. As you internalize these truths, they will become a natural part of what you believe, and therefore, they will "rewire" your brain.

Say with me:

- *"I am deeply loved by God, and I live my life authentically by loving Him and others around me. My heart is moved with love and compassion for the broken and hurting.*

- *I am a child who is so adored by my Father in Heaven. He has given me authority to administer mercy and justice for the poor.*

- *I am fully receiving the power and the baptism of the Holy Spirit.*

- *I am blessed and walking in all the gifts that God wants to activate in me.*

- *I am walking in the fulfillment of every promise God has for my life.*

- *I am overturning the demonic tactics that the enemy has put in my life through dead religion. I am walking out of every trap that has been set for me.*

- *I am unraveling the effects of dead religion in my life and in my family bloodline.*

- *I am receiving all the fruits and gifts of the spirit, using them to teach, exhort, and help others thrive."*

Scriptures to Meditate on

The following verses are key verses that will really help you fight the enemy when he tries to convince you that you still bound from the stronghold of dead religion. He is a liar! With the blood of Christ, you have been set free! The price has been paid! Speaking the Word of God out loud is a great way to remind yourself that you are victorious in Christ. Because the enemy hates the Word of God, He flees when we speak it out loud!

- James 1:27—Religion that God our Father accepts as pure and faultless is this: to look after orphans and widows in their distress and to keep oneself from being polluted by the world.

- Proverbs 21:22—One who is wise can go up against the city of the mighty and pull down the stronghold in which they trust.

- 2 Corinthians 10:3–5—For though we live in the world, we do not wage war as the world does. The weapons we fight with are not the weapons of the world. On the contrary, they have divine power to demolish strongholds. We demolish arguments and every pretension that sets itself up against the knowledge of God, and we take captive every thought to make it obedient to Christ.

- Hebrews 12:28—Therefore, since we are receiving a kingdom that cannot be shaken, let us be thankful, and so worship God acceptably with reverence and awe.

- 2 Timothy 3:5 (ESV)—...having the appearance of godliness, but denying its power. Avoid such people.

- Proverbs 31:8–9—Speak up for those who cannot speak for themselves, for the rights of all who are destitute. Speak up and judge fairly; defend the rights of the poor and needy.
- Proverbs 22:16 (ESV)—Whoever oppresses the poor to increase his own wealth, or give to the rich, will only come to poverty.
- 1 Corinthians 2:4—My message and my preaching were not with wise and persuasive words, but with a demonstration of the Spirit's power.

Great work! You are free in Christ! If, over time, you are looking for one more step, and you feel ready to go even deeper with the Lord, you can pray to receive the Baptism of the Holy Spirit. If you want to learn more about the baptism of the Holy Spirit, I invite you to review the following passages: Luke 3:16, Acts 8:15–19, Acts 19:6 and 1 Corinthians 12:4,6–11. You could also ask someone to pray with you who has received and understands the Baptism of the Holy Spirit.

Closing Prayer

"Father, I take authority back from the enemy. Father, I ask You to take dominion and authority over the stronghold of dead religion that has been operating in my life. I also ask that You set me free. I ask, Father God, that You not allow dead religion to bear fruit in my life ever again. Jesus, bind dead religion and strip it of its power. I invite you, Lord of Hosts, and Your warrior angels to dismantle and uproot dead religion and all of its assaults against my life and my family. Father God, carry this stronghold of dead religion out of my life now. I command this stronghold to go to the place Jesus sends you and to never return, in the name of Jesus Christ of Nazareth.

Father, I give you permission to rewire my brain and change my thinking concerning this stronghold of dead religion. Your Word says I have the mind of Christ, (1 Corinthians 2:16); therefore, I shall have it. Thank You for Your goodness and Your faithfulness. I apply the blood of Jesus to my mind and my emotions from this day forward. In Jesus' name I pray. Amen."

PERFORMANCE

"When you stop expecting people to be perfect, you can like them for who they are."[6]*— Donald Miller*

MY STORY

As I entered this land of the free and home of the brave at age six, I did not feel free, and I sure did not feel brave. I was broken, scared, and not sure who to trust. I started to question my worth. Like many, as I grew up, I wondered: *Am I loved, or even lovable? Am I enough?*

Two years before I came to the U.S., my parents had sent me to live with their friends in India so that I would become more disciplined. These caretakers in India believed that stern discipline was part of training a child. I agree that discipline is important, but I can say that the discipline I faced was severe. I was spanked throughout the day because I hadn't learned the basics in self-care. As I mentioned in the last chapter, at my grandmother's house, the place I had previously lived, I had servants taking care of my needs. Therefore, when I moved into this home with my parents' friends, the realization that I needed to do things for myself was a great shift for me. In this new environment, I made what were considered mistakes without affirmation of my value when I got things right. I learned to make my bed perfectly, to brush my teeth until they were shining, to dress in a timely manner, and to get things done systematically. In that year, I think I attained a level of personal discipline for which I am grateful that I still maintain to this day.

As an Asian Indian growing up first in India and then in the U.S., I learned to be driven to be the best and the top at whatever I did, especially in school. I wanted to succeed so badly because I came from a country where if you are poor, you are looked down on, discriminated against, and dishonored. I did not want to be either poor or dishonored. I'll explain more about this cultural Indian mindset in the section, "Exposing the Stronghold."

When I say I was determined to be the top of the class, I am not exaggerating. I believed I had to get a 100% on every assignment or test. If you are not Asian, you may be thinking this level of determination sounds crazy or over-the-top, but it was normal in my household. My parents did not voice this expectation often, yet I knew this level of perfection was expected. Overall, I found school work easy, especially English, except for the big obstacle that I had to overcome, which was the pronunciation of words in American English. I had only experienced British English in India. I had learned to read both British English and my native language, Malayalam, by the age of four. In first grade, I received lower grades in English, especially tests that involved identifying syllables. I would get out of school, put all my papers in my backpack, and walk home. I remember one day going home and showing my mom what I received on the English paper, which was an A, but it was a low A. I remember her disappointed look as she said, "Why did you not get

100?" I already had high expectations of myself, but the shame from my mother's disappointment only added to the pressure I felt. I was so afraid of her disapproval that from that point on that I decided I would throw away anything that was not a 100%. I only showed her the perfect papers. This pressure was the beginning of a performance stronghold taking root in my life.

Before I go on with my story, I'd like to share how I define this particular stronghold. **A performance stronghold puts ungodly pressure to perform perfectly without mistakes or failures**. When this performance stronghold is at work, we measure our worth based on our accomplishments. This stronghold creates a false sense of fulfillment measured only by perfection.

This stronghold, which had originated in India continued in me partially because my parents' Indian values were reinforced in Asian Indian communities our family was a part of in the U.S. It was natural for my parents as Asian Indians to spend time with like-minded people. We had events with this community at least once a month, sometimes more. Honestly, I dreaded going to these social gatherings because if you meet an Indian, the first thing that he or she will ask you is, "What do you DO?" or "How are your studies coming along?" These questions are asked to size up what level of achievement you have or to measure your success. Even though before these conversations I felt like I was doing pretty well in life, I was so frustrated with these questions. I would walk away feeling unsuccessful, sad, or depressed—I felt like I didn't measure up to others' expectations of me.

Because the performance stronghold was so prevalent in my home, it was normal at the dinner table to be compared to one of my parents' friends' children. Asian parents think it inspires their children to perform better by comparing them to other friends or family. This practice actually created more shame, guilt, and insecurity, which, in turn, made me perform at a much lower level than my actual capacity. At my house as we ate dinner, the normal conversation when I was in high school would go something like this:

"So, Sarah, how did you do on your ACT?"

"Well, I got a 28."

"Oh, why did you not get a 36? Preethi got 36. She just got a full scholarship to Princeton and graduated valedictorian."

With this type of conversation as a normal part of my life, I spent many years comparing myself to others. I often felt anxious and insecure about myself and my level of performance in school. These feelings were present in my friendships as well. When I fell into the comparison trap with my friends, I was secretly jealous of their talents. I was super competitive with grades or in seeking the highest-class officer position to receive affirmation. I also came off as conceited. Despite how I thought of myself or how I came across, underneath it all, I was an ordinary person functioning under an extraordinary amount of pressure.

As I have shared, I believed that I had to do everything perfectly, otherwise I would have been punished, shamed, or caused disappointment. I quickly accepted the idea that if I did not excel in the areas expected of me, I would not be celebrated, and possibly, I would have been rejected. I had a deep longing in my soul to be loved genuinely and unconditionally—like all humans do. I was unaware, however, of the depth of this need to be loved. The accumulation of continuously falling short and not being perfect led me to the conclusion that I was unworthy of love and acceptance if I did not do all things in life flawlessly. Therefore, perfection and performance equaled love and acceptance in my life. For many years, I only understood conditional love based on how well I did in school or at work. Conditional love assigns terms, restrictions, or rules on the giving of love. Unconditional love, on the other hand, is boundless, given freely, without a requirement of repayment. I know that the intention of my parents was to love me at all times. This cultural and generational stronghold, however, hindered them from loving me for who God designed me to be without conditions. Their propensity, then, was to show me love when I performed well in school, college, or even in my career. The comparison comments made me feel that I was not good enough, smart enough, or capable enough whenever I had great challenges ahead of me. I carried much self-doubt about my abilities from childhood to adult years. I took on challenges doing my best, but I was not confident in myself. I carried this mindset even into my mid-30s.

As I came of age, I was desperately trying to do what my family and my culture expected: to go to college, get an education, get a great job, and be successful. These were good aspirations, but I could feel myself, at times, begin to crack under the pressure of achievement even though I was on a road to gain money, success, and a sense of security.

After I completed my education, the performance stronghold maintained its grip in my career in the medical field as a physical therapist. I felt pressure to get as many patients into my schedule as possible to increase the bottom line of the corporation. Although I was quickly rewarded with a promotion directing a physical therapy clinic for a large corporation, I had ongoing stress to generate money for the company. I had to fight for what was most important to my heart—providing the best patient care.

Enduring extreme discipline in India as a young child led to unintended consequences that plagued and even paralyzed me into my adult years. This ongoing push to perform perfectly contributed to me losing my child-like wonder and creativity. Only recently did I realize how much I love this childlike part of me. Most people who know me would say that I am very serious. My family jokes with me now because I have a history of being so serious that my children would cry in the early years when I tried to make a light-hearted joke. They were in shock as this side of me opened up, and they didn't know how to process my attempt to be funny. Honestly, I did not realize how serious I was until I married Scott, my happy-go-lucky husband who constantly jokes. Although having fun is one of his life's missions, his happy nature would actually make me angry!

When God called me into full-time ministry and pastoring, I thought I was going to be running into a safe place where I could be free from performance. Boy was I wrong! I was shocked when I discovered the prevailing performance stronghold was in the world of the Christian church. The performance stronghold was just as bad there as it had been in the corporate world and in my academic life. In fact, the pain and wounds from the performance stronghold seemed even more difficult because a church community is where I expected to have the freedom to be unique without the pressure to perform. Instead, I felt an unhealthy pressure to increase my followers on social media, to add more speaking engagements, and to invite the most renowned ministry or worship leader to our church to increase our relevance. These performance-driven activities are not where our priorities ought to be in ministry.

Through every area of my life, I have learned that as much as we want unconditional love from our parents, spouses, friends, colleagues, or fellow ministry workers, they won't be able to satisfy that longing and need we have for perfect love. Only God has the

ability to love and accept us at all times in both our successes and
failures.

FINDING MY FREEDOM

In my mid-30s, my role as a wife, pastor, friend, and daughter was exhausting me. I lived my life under this performance stronghold, trying to do everything perfectly and successfully, but I was always falling short. Admittedly, I took people-pleasing bait that often comes with a performance stronghold in the early years of ministry. One day, I ended up crawling into my bedroom closet, screaming at the top of my lungs telling God that I could not do things the same way anymore. All of these roles were too heavy for me, and I was weary. I felt like I was having a mental breakdown because of the amount of pressure that I was living under as I tried to please everybody else around me to prove my value. I was also living with the fear of being rejected if I couldn't live up to other people's expectations of me. I finally came to the end of myself.

At that moment on the closet floor, I encountered God's deep love for me. I felt God, as a loving Father, break off this unhealthy mindset and stronghold of performance. I had previously tried to do so much for God. I had tried to perform so many good works to earn favor with God. I had been operating in a works-based mindset. I also felt the weight of being a pastor and trying to meet everybody's expectations of me, along with the possibility of failing them. I wanted this approval so much that I had an unhealthy fear of human opinion. This fear is also called the "fear of man." I felt like I was constantly disappointing someone. That day in my bedroom closet, when I spent time with the Father alone, quiet, and in His presence, I asked Him hard questions:

What do you think about me? Am I enough? Would you still love me if I didn't do anything else for you?

In His mercy, God gently whispered:

"Sarah, I have loved you from the moment I thought of you. You are loved, cherished, and adored. There is nothing you can do on Earth to earn this love. I love everything about you. You are enough just as you are. If you don't do anything for me for the rest of your life, I will still love you."

That day, when I cried out to God for help, the driven, disciplined, perfectionistic human I had been was dismantled and rearranged. It was as if my DNA changed! How I saw myself and how I lived from that day on was different. When I think about this encounter, I think about when Saul was on his way to Damascus, living his life persecuting all the followers of Jesus. But then he was blinded by the light of Christ. Three days later, the scales fell off his eyes, and he was baptized in the Holy Spirit. His name and character changed, and he became one of the most impactful apostles. While I might not have been persecuting Christians like Saul before this dramatic event in my life, I was persecuting myself with judgments, looking through the lens of my failures and flaws. On the day I cried out to the Lord, I was finally freed from crippling self-judgment!

After this encounter with the Lord, I felt like a caged bird set free! I was set free from feeling like I had to be smart enough, good enough, perfect enough, friendly enough, and religious enough to be loved my family, church, friends—and even God. I learned that I am valued and loved, not based on what I do or the roles I hold but for who I am from the inside out. From that day forward, my identity of knowing who I am in Christ has been secure and anchored in truth that God's love for me is unfailing.

God knows my name, and He sees me and loves me. I am significant, and I am important and valuable—not because of my achievements or how big Scott and I grow our church, but because

God sees my faith and calls me a beloved daughter. Our worth is not based on doing; our worth is based on being. All of my passion and sustainability for life now comes from a place of knowing that I am rooted and grounded in His great love for me. From that overflow, I serve, disciple, train, and deliver people out of darkness, lies, and schemes. I am able to show them the Father's love, light, and truth. I have to say: although I lived my early life under this performance stronghold, I refuse to allow the stronghold to sabotage my future. If I continued to buy into this performance trap, I would not have met nor had the privilege of investing in so many beautiful people, including my family and my church family. Nor would I have had the ability to serve and connect to so many in my city.

I would say next to accepting Jesus Christ as my Lord and Savior, the encounter in my closet, where God whispered my worth, was the most life-changing moment I have ever experienced. I started to understand that I am so loved by Him not because of my works, but because of who God is. He loves me unconditionally. In life, as I freely received this unconditional love, I began to notice that I was not so hard on myself anymore; I did not demand perfection in all things. I gave myself permission to make mistakes.

I realized that as I became less judgmental of myself, I became less judgmental of others as well. I was also less harsh on my friends, family, and staff. I was able to celebrate my friends and peers successes instead of being envious and jealous. I focused on doing my best in whatever I was called to do, whether cleaning my kitchen, taking care of my church family, or taking care of my immediate family and my children. Instead of thinking, *I am slow and uncapable,* if I left my dishes in the sink for a time or didn't clean up perfectly, I would think, *Sarah, you had a long day, and you still got that kitchen cleaned somewhat in the midst of such a hectic day. It's okay that it's not perfect. It's great because you are doing your best.* I also learned that how we treat ourselves will directly affect how we treat others.

To help you more fully see the widespread effects of my transformation, I'd like to share a bit more about my background pastoring this community. I started ministry work at the age of 26, soon after I got married. I was ordained as a pastor in my mid-30s. Since that time until the present time as I write, I have co-led a church we planted in the inner-city of Nashville called Harvest Sound. We started this church wanting to be the hands and feet of Jesus because we saw so many hurting and suffering in the devastated parts of American cities. As I have mentioned, these areas are known as inner cities. They are also called "Section 8" projects. God had told my husband and I to build and handle church like a family—not a corporation. Listening to Him was so fruitful—both in their lives and in ours! I came alive as I spent one-on-one time with these children and young adults, diving into their hearts, hearing their stories, and seeing the treasure in each one.

Only two weeks after my encounter in the closet with Father God, something unusual happened that I will never forget. Before this encounter, as I have mentioned, I had been feeling like failure as a pastor, and I was overwhelmed with caring for this community with hundreds of single moms and their children living in an area full of drugs, violence, and prostitution. After my encounter, I felt the complete opposite—I was full of peace and equipped to serve by His power. Soon I began to see the effects not only in me but also in our community. One of the first most amazing effects happened in the dance school I started. We taught hip-hop and ballet for kids ages 5 to 18. At the beginning of class, we would warm-up using Christian worship music. One particular night, I felt a supernatural peace in the room as we played worship music. A holy hush and presence entered the room. As I started to look around, all I saw was the room covered with children on the ground in tears. These children had previously been some of the most difficult, obstinate, rebellious ones I had ever encountered! Then I heard one intense, gut-wrenching wailing after another.

I did not know what was coming, as I had never seen this behavior with these kids. I asked each one of them, "What is wrong? Why are you crying?" All they could say is, "We see ABBA." They each said it over and over. *Abba* is the Hebrew word for *father*. They were all encountering the Heavenly Father's unconditional love for the first time. I know this revelation was supernatural because they had not ever learned this word *Abba*. In addition, most of the kids in this class were fatherless. The result of this supernatural revelation to their hearts was astonishing! Their personalities became calmer, kinder, more respectful, and happier. If these children can encounter the Father's love, so can anyone!

About 12 years into full-time ministry and having this encounter with Abba, I realized I had to stop going to selected ministry meetings where a performance mindset was reinforced over and over again. I knew I also had to focus on what God had told me to do, which was to disciple and invest in a handful of young people so that they could make an impact and become what God had designed them to be. I knew to not underestimate the power of discipling and investing into a small group of people—or even just one person. Jesus himself discipled only 12, and they turned the world upside down. Therefore, we decided to simply invest in people one-on-one, no matter what class or culture they came from. We invested in people from all backgrounds and created a safe place for all races and social classes. God told me not to worry about growing the number of people in our church, but instead, to grow the hearts of the people.

As I simply invested my time and resources, I saw some of the most extraordinary people emerge as they became strong, steadfast, and mature, grounded in their faith and in their identities. An example of a person coming into her own was a young lady I met when she was 18 years old. She had lived a promiscuous, drug-filled, rebellious life during her teen years after her father passed away from cancer when she was only 13. Her name is Courtney Cordes. She attended our ministry leadership school called Harvest Sound Intensive. Then she went through our discipleship program and eventually joined us on staff. As we helped anchor her faith in the Word of God and His great love for her, the broken parts of her heart become more healed and whole. The outcome was that she became one of the most admired and adored people I have ever known. She was widely known for her extreme love for God and people. She used her worship and teaching gifts to lead people to JESUS and to help them get to know Him more. She has graduated to Heaven, but her extraordinary legacy of compassion for the weak and vulnerable, along with her extravagant love for all races and classes—rich, poor, young, and old—will forever mark the lives of all of those she touched, including mine. She finished her race on Earth brilliantly. If I had not broken free from the stronghold of performance, I would not have had the insight or capacity to patiently draw out the gold in individuals like Courtney.

EXPOSING THE STRONGHOLD

This section will help you see the potential trap of the performance stronghold, both for yourself and for society at large.

Without an understanding God's unconditional love, the lie that we have to perform perfectly may continue to grow in our minds, just like it did in my story. This lie grows with failure, and we all fail at times. With failure comes shame, guilt, and ultimately, rejection. This performance stronghold—a result of believing this lie that we have to be perfect for an extended period of time without failure—not only causes shame and other negative emotions, but the performance stronghold actually prevents growth because growth and creativity often arise the most profoundly out of failure.

The motivation behind the performance mindset is usually a good or noble one. People want to be the best at whatever they do. But when the desire to be great becomes a controlling mindset driving toward perfectionism, it is toxic to us and those around us. Through my experiences, I have realized that this stronghold is widespread. You may have experienced the oppression caused by this performance stronghold as well.

To begin to determine if you are under the influence of this stronghold, ask yourself the following questions:

- Do you believe that no matter what you do, you will never be good enough, fast enough, or smart enough to compete?
- Do you look at social media and think that you are a failure, even if you have done a full day's work that day?
- Are you perpetually comparing yourself to others?

If you answered yes to these questions, you may be in bondage to this stronghold. You will have a chance to more fully assess your life and to use the tools to secure your freedom at the end of this chapter. First, however, I want you to see how widespread and devastating the effects of this stronghold are. I've found this information helps people realize that they are not alone—and you aren't either! If we all do our part to dismantle this stronghold, the entire world could change!

In India

As I alluded to in my story, in Asian Indian culture, the performance stronghold permeates all of society. Education is valued because students in the top of the class in school usually get good jobs and break out of poverty. For the middle- to upper-class Asian Indians, the goal, which is understood by anyone in that culture, is to be ranked number one, whether in kindergarten or high school. The belief is that if you attain the best scores, you will get into the best universities and then get the best jobs.

This performance stronghold is so prevalent in India that the country's suicide rates are at their highest during exam times among students. This sobering reality is often attributed to the intense pressure from family and cultural expectations. In fact, the National Crime Records Bureau in India has gone as far as creating a statistical category for suicides caused by academic failure. This stronghold, derived from an unhealthy performance mindset, drives students to take their lives rather than face the shame of missing the high standard set for them. In fact, in 2021, 13,089 students committed suicide, driven by "failure in examination."[7]

This pressure doesn't stop once a person is out of school. The societal pressure then shifts for people to be highly productive. People are judged by what they do, not by their innate personalities or who they are. The pressure to perform is not only found in education and career, but also, this pressure is reinforced through Hindu religious beliefs. As I've mentioned, Hinduism, India's main religion, permeates the culture with its caste system that creates the country's social classes. The type of professions Asian Indians choose are mostly determined by these social class expectations. In the social class my family was born into, some of the most acceptable professions to choose are medicine, law, engineering, accountancy, or IT (information technology).

Each caste is required to perform the duties and laws of the religion and therefore gain "good Karma." The level of performance associated with people's duties will enable them to be reincarnated into the next life as well as to be reborn into someone or something better than they were previously. Failure to meet this "good Karma" would mean that people could be demoted in the next life, and each person who fails could come back as a cow, monkey, or possibly even a fly. As we have seen, the pressure to excel in performance in India comes from the religious, educational, and financial sectors of society. Therefore, the performance stronghold is widespread in India. As we are about to see, however, Indian culture is not an anomaly.

All Over the World

The comparison trap and intense pressure on performance doesn't just happen in Asian Indian families—it happens to one degree or another in all cultures. How many people around the world are on paths chosen for us by parents, friends, or cultural expectations? Parents comparing their children to others is painful. We who see this comparison modeled then go on to cause more damage as we compare ourselves to our peers, basing our significance and defining our level of success on how we rank ourselves.

Not only does this performance stronghold have its grip on families in all ethnicities as children are raised, but its influence is evident across various spheres of society, including athletics, families, business, media/entertainment, and even in the church.

We hear of athletes using body-altering steroids that may later damage their hearts in order to perform. We see people working themselves to death, allowing their health, their emotional life, and their relationships to suffer to get to the top of the corporate ladder. We see addiction to drugs and alcohol in the lives of celebrities, actors, and musicians in media and entertainment because they feel like they can't measure up to the image that has been created for their lives.

In the Church

Because Christianity is based on loving Christ and one another, it can be surprising for people—just as it was for me—that a performance stronghold finds its way inside the church. When we end up comparing ourselves or even competing with other ministers, worship leaders, or ministries instead of loving others, we find ourselves disillusioned. I have found that in some churches there is much pressure and emphasis on performance. This pressure can overshadow what God wants, which is simply for all of us to be faithful and to do our best with what He has entrusted to us. One of the performance-based lies that may develop into a stronghold if the lie is perpetually believed is that the more people attend a pastor's church, the more successful that pastor is. But if we build the church based on a performance mentality, we will build the church based on a pastor or worship leader's popularity and fame rather than the NAME of JESUS, who is looking for us to be humble and faithful. In the "Dead Religion" chapter, I shared about how Jesus, when He was on Earth, rebuked the religious leaders who were more concerned about what people thought of them than what God thought about them.

Sadly, some of our modern-day churches are run like businesses, and pastors have pressure to manage the corporation instead of watching over and tending to their church members' hearts and lives. In reality, a church's effectiveness is based on the strength and the quality of the people—not the quantity of the people. The Americanized Western model of church has become distorted, I believe. For many years, the measure of success in some American churches was based on world-renowned speakers and a stage with lights and fog machines. Some in church culture put much emphasis on the church "show," which includes how sophisticated the lights and sound system are. The comfort of the seats, and other external, cosmetic facets are also what those in a performance stronghold tend to notice. These performance-based measures only lead to competition and jealousy, along with a false, worldly sense of success.

Even secular culture notices effects of the performance stronghold in the church. I recently heard a state government official in America say that he was tired of mega churches giving micro messages to people. Many are coming to church not to worship Jesus but because of a famous speaker or worship leader. In some churches, people are consistently fed the "dessert." When someone gives them a nourishing and sustainable message (in other words, the meat), they don't want it because the "sweet" messages have spoiled their appetites for anything life changing. The church and its leadership are called to be salt and brilliant light to a dark world. As churches and their leadership teams come out of agreement with the stronghold of performance, they will fulfill their true callings and they will be able to fulfill the command of being salt and light by loving God, loving each other, and loving the hurting, broken world.

ESCAPING THE STRONGHOLD

This section is your invitation to break free so you can live free.

A performance stronghold is probably one of the most difficult to break free from because it has penetrated all spheres of society to the point of acceptance as normal, even beneficial, behavior. It was so ingrained into my lifestyle, my mind, my opinions of others, my ministry, and my goals that I didn't know it was there. If I have discovered anything through the years about this topic, it is that **my performance mindset circumvented the unique mark I was created to leave here on Earth.**

We were not created to live from this performance mindset. We were designed by God to live in a mindset of excellence. Bill Johnson, pastor at Bethel Church in Redding, California, discusses what excellence is and isn't. He says, "Perfectionism is the counterfeit of excellence. Excellence is Kingdom, while perfectionism is religion. Whatever you do, do it with all you might, and as unto the Lord. That is excellence."[5]

Excellence flows out of rest and peace knowing that we do not have to prove ourselves to anyone. I give all of us permission to stop comparing ourselves to others, whether we serve as a parent, student, musician, artist, athlete, entertainer, politician, business owner, educator, government official, or ministry leader. All we have to do is focus on becoming the best version of ourselves! As I've mentioned, this comparison mindset is prevalent across all walks of life: business, religion, politics, entertainment, athletics, education, and even in family life and parenting. We have to break free from the comparison trap so that we can live out our original design, making the best use of the gifts and talents that are unique to us. No one else can take the unique roles that God created for each one of us.

I invite all of us to exchange performance for excellence. When we are doing our best at our jobs, school, sports, studies, or whatever is set before us, we will be exceptional. When our hearts are set to do life with excellence and not perfection, we will naturally grow because we can receive feedback or correction without getting defensive. The performance stronghold makes us so hard on ourselves that when we receive feedback or correction, we feel like we are a failure or like we don't measure up. Let's instead remember that failure fosters growth. Let's give ourselves the ability to try things, and the room to learn if we make mistakes. Some of the greatest inventors failed many times before they created inventions that we rely on to this day. Thomas Edison, who invented the light bulb, failed thousands of times before he created a version of the lightbulb that worked correctly.

Our God-given identities are not rooted in what we do, but they are based on knowing who we are at our core as individuals. Our unique selves are designed by God so that we make a difference in this life. Our identities are found when we discover what God says about us, not based on what the world or our parents, friends, coaches, teachers, and bosses have labeled us or who they expect us to be. So, I invite each one of us to sit with God to go through the upcoming sections: "Performance Identifiers" and "Reflection Questions." Get silent and let Him speak.

Some of you may have felt that God has never spoken to you individually. Perhaps you have not known how to access His voice. Hearing His voice is just tuning into how you are wired and silencing the voice of the enemy, who is usually speaking in his native tongue of lies. Hearing God's voice may correspond to your learning style—if you learn visually, you might see things through pictures; if you learn kinesthetically, you may engage all our senses to experience Him; if you learn audibly, you might hear a word, a phrase—more with spiritual or natural ears. God may give you a particular scripture, or you might sense or feel something in your spirit—the place where each of us come to know God. Sometimes I feel something in my gut or belly. However we receive communication from God, we can trust His Word because it will confirm the truth and bring us peace.

To truly experience a healthy version of a relationship with Jesus without a performance stronghold, we will need to learn to trust Him unconditionally no matter what is going on in our lives. He will accept us just as we are. He loves us just as we are.

When we receive unconditional love, we have the capacity and strength to endure and overcome the challenges that life throws at us, including losses of a job, a friendship, or a relationship, as well as the devastation we may face if we fail an exam or suffer a financial hardship. When we receive unconditional love, we are not measured by our level of work, our achievements, or things we do. We are seen and accepted just as we are with nothing to prove.

God loves us unconditionally because He created us! We do not have to be a great athlete, good-looking, popular, intellectual, successful, or wealthy. His love is not rooted in any of these things! His love is solely rooted in what Jesus did for each of us on the cross, which made it possible for God to be reconciled to each of us. Receiving all that God has for us takes complete and unconditional trust. Our relationship with Him is actually a covenant (an unbreakable agreement) based on trust. When we invite God in and surrender our lives to Jesus, we receive His love, which is always abounding. We don't have to earn this love because it is not based on our achievements, but instead, it is based on our relationship with Him.

What's amazing is that His love has healing powers. What I so love about Father God is that He has such a deep love for all people—each person is His favorite! He longs to see each of us discover and live out our true identities; He doesn't want us to try to be an imitation of someone else. In fact, that effort will always fail because He didn't create us to be imitators. He created us to be uniquely who He envisioned us to be.

As we deepen our relationships with Father God, also know that human love is not enough. It can never satisfy us. No matter how devoted or sincere, it is still human. God's love, on the other hand, is never-ending. Our love for family or children is like a drop in the ocean compared to God's love. God's love is like the ocean. His love cannot be earned—it is a free gift. When we receive this free gift, we also freely receive the inheritance which allows us to rule and reign on Earth. When each of us understands and receives the depth of His love, we are adopted into His royal family! When each of us receives this free gift of love, we are given freedom. We no longer need to earn approval by being good enough, popular enough, or smart enough. We are good enough, popular enough, and smart enough because we belong to God. Therefore, we can become free from performance and the things we do. We can rest in the value and worth He has placed on us.

We were created by Him so that we could have true, authentic connections with Him because of His great love for us. Let me share what I've learned about His great love: it is not fractured; it keeps promises; it is not insecure. He doesn't tear our hearts to pieces; He only takes the broken pieces and makes them whole. He will never leave us nor forsake us.

It is time to restore what has been stolen from us. Let's remove ourselves from any ways we have aligned with this stronghold of performance. Our end goal is to be excellence-driven with our identity rooted in Christ. In the next section, we will assess whether each of us have a performance stronghold operating in our lives. Let me provide encouragement before we move on—there is nothing to fear about this process—even if we feel completely scared or broken right now.

God is close to the brokenhearted. And God has big plans to free us from any heartbreak we have endured—for our good, for our impact in the world, and most importantly, for His glory! Loving others well first starts with receiving unconditional love from God. I believe when we receive a personal breakthrough, not only is it for us individually, but also, it is for those in our spheres of influence. Our newfound freedom can be passed on to the many generations that come after us. The decisions we make today can affect our descendants for years to come.

So, take God's hand, pray, and let Him continue to transform you—so that you can break free and live free!

ASSESSING YOURSELF

Performance Mindset Identifiers

For each stronghold, 20 identifiers are listed. As you read, put a check mark by the ones you feel apply to you. Each check mark will be considered one point. Add up the check marks, which will give you the total points for this stronghold. By the end of this book, you will be able to rank which stronghold needs the most attention first by the greatest number of points. (Most people have some of each; if this happens to you, don't be discouraged. God will enable you to break free of every stronghold—it just may take some time.)

1. I tend to try to please people.
2. I do not allow myself permission to make mistakes.
3. I tend to judge myself based on my level of performance.
4. I feel value based on how people treat me.
5. I obtain value from jobs, titles, and materials gains such as houses or cars, or popularity metrics such as social media followers.
6. I feel the need to prove talent or impress people.
7. I tend to boast about education level or accolades.
8. I tend to feel stuck in a cycle of comparing myself to others, so I live in a place of inadequacy and self-rejection.
9. I feel exhausted from trying to meet expectations perfectly.
10. I feel shame over not being "enough" (smart enough, beautiful enough, successful enough, rich enough, important enough).
11. I tend to be affected by the opinion of what friends, family, or my co-workers think about me.
12. I tend to think of myself as a perfectionist and demand perfection from myself.

13. I tend to have a hard time receiving feedback or criticism.

14. I tend to be afraid of what people think about me.

15. I tend to live for the praise or accolades of my family, friends, or peers.

16. I tend to judge others based on their achievements.

17. I need to impress others by what I do and my level of performance.

18. I feel like I need to earn God's favor.

19. I expect and demand perfection from the people in my world.

20. I tend to function as an overachiever, no matter the task.

Reflection Questions

Take a few moments to get quiet and think about the following reflection questions and write your answers in a journal.

1. Have you personally encountered the performance stronghold in your life? How did it negatively affect you?

2. What symptoms of the performance stronghold have you noticed in your life?

3. Was there a part of my story that you related to in your own life?

4. On a scale of 0 to 10, how would you rate the performance stronghold affecting your life?

5. What are two action steps you can put in place to live your life to come out from under this performance stronghold and live excellence-driven?

STEPPING INTO YOUR FREEDOM

If you recognize this performance mindset in yourself, the following are some clear steps to take so that you dismantle this stronghold that has tried to hold you captive. The first step is to repent, which means to turn completely in the opposite direction of it.

Repent

Pray with me:

"God I'm so sorry. I'm repent for every way I partnered with the performance mindset and allowed this stronghold to rule my life, my decisions, and my thinking patterns. Your Word says to take every thought captive to the obedience of Christ. I am taking this performance stronghold captive, and I no longer allow it to ensnare me."

Renounce

To renounce a stronghold is to break agreement with toxic beliefs that have formed a stronghold. When we renounce something, we make a declaration that we no longer affiliate with that system of beliefs.

Break agreement with the following statements that apply to you. I break agreement with the stronghold of performance because:

- I have demanded perfection for myself and others.
- I have critically judged others.
- I have tried to earn approval by being good enough popular enough smart enough.

- I have placed my value and worth on humans instead of God.
- I have engaged in pleasing people behavior.
- I have not given myself or others permission to fail.
- I have been stuck in cycles of comparison.
- I have had feelings of inadequacy and self-rejection.
- I have felt shame from not being enough.
- I have had continuous concern about how others see me.
- I have been unable to receive criticism.
- I have been stuck in a cycle of overachieving.
- I have a difficult time admitting weakness; I have thought acknowledging that I'm wrong makes me vulnerable.

Declare with me:

"I renounce and break all agreements I have made with the stronghold of performance. Specifically, I renounce the beliefs of performance found in the statements above that I just broke agreement with. I am so sorry, God, for coming into agreement with performance, and I'm sorry for how I have lived my life based on the effects of it. Please forgive me, Father God, for not consecrating a life of excellence to You. I want to walk in my original design without pressure to perform from now on."

Release

Pray with me:

"Father God, I release this performance stronghold and place it at Your feet. Break me free from all the ways it has affected my life from conception until this moment…Remove any of the ways the stronghold of performance has affected how I have treated myself or

others as I have demanded perfection and placed judgement on them or myself. I choose this day no longer to compare myself to others or be harshly critical of myself and others. Today I choose to fully receive You and live consecrating my life and future to You. I receive the power of Your blood to wash and renew me."

Restore

Pray with me:

"Father God, what do You want to give me in place of performance and perfectionism? What is my identity in You? Show me the value You have given me."

Rewire

- *"I am deeply loved by God, and I live my life excellence driven. He has given me my value not based on what I do or what I achieve but based on my relationship with Him and His deep love for me.*

- *I am blessed as I no longer compare myself to others, but instead, I live out the best version of me because there is no one like me.*

- *I am enough. What is inside me is original, and I am walking in the gifts that God designed and wants to activate in me.*

- *I am walking in the fulfillment of every promise God has for my life. I am not afraid to try new things. Even if I fail, I am learning and growing.*

- *I am no longer pushed to perform for man's approval, but rather, I do what God says. I am overturning the demonic tactics that the enemy has put in my life through performance. I am walking out of every trap that has been set for me.*

- *I am unraveling the effects of the stronghold of performance in my life and in my family bloodline.*
- *I am living out my best life fulfilling the original design and purpose God put in me."*

Scripture to Meditate on

Now it's your turn. Read these scriptures, and if a few jump out to you, write a prayer or declaration based on the scripture.

- Proverbs 29:25—Fearing people is a dangerous trap, but trusting the Lord means safety.
- Colossians 3:23—Whatever you do, work heartily, as for the Lord and not for men.
- Romans 8:38–39—For I am sure that neither death nor life, nor angels nor rulers, nor things present nor things to come, nor powers, nor height nor depth, nor anything else in all creation, will be able to separate us from the love of God in Christ Jesus our Lord.
- Psalms 118:8—It is better to take refuge in the Lord than to trust in man.
- Ephesians 3:16–19—I pray that out of his glorious riches he may strengthen you with power through his Spirit in your inner being, so that Christ may dwell in your hearts through faith, and I pray that you be being rooted and established in love, may have power, together with all the Lord's holy people to grasp how wide and long and high and deep is the love of Christ, and to know this love that surpasses knowledge—that you may be filled to measure of all the fullness of God.

- Romans 5:8—But God demonstrates his own love for us in this while we were still sinners Christ died for us.
- Philippians 4:13—I can do all things through him who strengthens me.

Closing Prayer

"Father, I take authority back from the enemy. Father, I ask You to take dominion and authority over the stronghold of performance that has been operating in my life, and I ask that You set me free. I ask, Father God, that You not allow this stronghold to bear fruit in my life ever again. Jesus, bind performance stronghold and strip it of its power. I invite you, Lord of Hosts, and Your warrior angels to dismantle and uproot the stronghold of performance and all of its assaults against my life and my family. Father God, carry this stronghold of performance out of my life now. I command this stronghold to go to the place Jesus sends you and to never return, in the name of Jesus Christ of Nazareth.

Father I give you permission to rewire my brain and change my thinking concerning this stronghold of performance. You Word says I have the mind of Christ (I Corinthians 2:16); therefore, I shall have it.. Thank You for Your goodness and Your faithfulness. I apply the blood of Jesus to my mind and my emotions from this day forward. In Jesus' name I pray. Amen."

KNOWLEDGE

*The fear of the Lord is the beginning of knowledge, but fools despise wisdom and instruction—Proverbs 1:7
Man's knowledge is futile—Psalms 94:11*

MY STORY

The blows of the knowledge stronghold had already taken a toll on me from the time of my birth because the effects of strongholds can be passed down generationally. My newlywed parents became pregnant with me only three months into their marriage. Along with my mother's pregnancy came the most prestigious, dream proposal for my parents. My father was offered a full scholarship to work on his doctorate in biomedical sciences in the United States. My mother also received a scholarship for her doctorate in microbiology. For my parents, who were young college professors in India, these scholarships were amazing opportunities that promised to provide long-term financial security. As I mentioned, my parents decided to leave me at only 12 months old in India with my widowed grandmother. I know that the heart of especially my father was to provide by pursuing this educational path, but that decision had a devastating effect on my life that left a deep fracture in my soul.

The burden was heavy for me physically, emotionally, and spiritually—although it took decades for the burden and bondage of this separation to be uncovered.

My education and pursuit of knowledge started in India at my grandmother's house. By age three, I had private tutors teaching me math and English. I have been told that I acted like a three-year-old getting educated; I gave my grandmother every excuse in the book not to sit down and study with my tutor. I would "just happen" to get a stomachache or feel sick many times when the tutor arrived at the house. By the age of four when I lived with my parent's friends, I was walking to school in India and doing lots of homework—but, as I mentioned in earlier chapters, I still got severely punished when I didn't do enough.

By the beginning of elementary school, I was finally reunited with my parents in Boston, Massachusetts. Up through sixth grade, I went to a public school and always ranked high in my class, getting all As. In seventh grade, I transferred to a private school called Wichita Collegiate School (WCS)in Kansas. This school was a college prep school with a great reputation. I was excited and able to go because I got a full headmaster's scholarship. The school was and still is really expensive. As I write, the tuition at WCS is about $21,000 a year for high school.

When I started seventh grade, most of my classmates were children of some of the wealthiest corporation owners in the U.S. These classmates had parents who wanted them to go to Ivy League schools. Most of my classmates had started kindergarten at WCS and were trained up in its rigorous program. I hadn't had as high of a level of academic knowledge and training when I started there in seventh. Therefore, I had to study daily from about 3:30 to 9:30 p.m. to keep up with the others. I wanted to be at the top of my class, and I enjoyed studying, so I didn't mind the work. When I started at WCS, I began feeling insecure because my identity was wrapped around my intelligence and driven by the performance stronghold that I discussed in the last chapter. As I mentioned, I began to overcompensate for my insecurity by acting prideful and boasting about my grades.

Despite my best efforts, my weaker academic areas were exposed at WCS. I was not a fast reader nor was I as quick to comprehend as others were. These weaknesses caused my ACT and SAT scores to be lower than my classmates because I could not read or answer quickly enough to get the highest scores. Nevertheless, I still tried to compensate by studying harder and longer, but my lack of confidence continued to grow. I still managed to get all As and went on to a public university in Tennessee to get my physical therapy degree. That field was also a highly competitive field. To be considered for an interview for admission to the program the year that I applied, students had to have an average GPA of 3.8 and higher. It was harder to get into physical therapy school than it was medical school because of the intensity of the competition; only 35 students were granted admission out of more than 1,000 applicants. I felt pressured to prove my intelligence to my peers and professors, and therefore, I became even more competitive. I felt resentment if any of my classmates scored higher than me on their exams. I did graduate from physical therapy school in the top percentile, and initially in my career, as I mentioned earlier, I ended up with a director's position for a physical therapy clinic in Franklin, Tennessee. At this point in my life, I had achieved a high level of success, partly driven by the need to prove that I was smart and successful. My success, however, was driven by a stronghold rooted in worldly knowledge.

Before I go further, I want to share my definition of this stronghold. The stronghold of knowledge is the fixation with acquiring knowledge apart from the all-knowing One—God.

Because knowledge was valued throughout the country of my birth, it is no surprise, as I have shared, that in my home, love and attention were based on how well I performed in school. This conditional love created an unhealthy competitive edge in me, driving me to constantly think about how I could get to the top. I would also judge the people around me. I even judged my friends if they were not as smart as I was, choosing my friends based on how smart I thought they were. I didn't say judgmental things out loud, but I certainly thought them. As I mentioned, I was obsessed with studying to compete with my peers. I didn't just want to be the top of my class. I wanted to prove to family and friends that I was intelligent and therefore worthy of their love and affirmation. I developed self-protective pride, which contributed to me devaluing people in my mind. I thought of myself as having a greater value than those who I perceived were not as smart as I was—and I thought this assigning of worth based on intellect was a normal way of thinking. Even with this superiority complex, my own self-worth was fragile and almost shattered growing up under the stronghold of knowledge.

Only recently did I realize how profoundly the quest for education had affected not only myself but also my mother. A few years ago, my mother's mental capacity was deteriorating. She had been diagnosed with dementia. Thankfully, she has been healed! But during the time of her cognitive difficulties, one memory continued to surface. She kept bringing up the time she had to leave me when I was only one to pursue educational scholarships in the U.S. As she relived this memory, she expressed the deep ache she felt about having to leave and not getting a chance to raise me until years later. Before my mother's cognitive struggles, I hadn't known how much grief this decision had caused her. Hearing my mother's journey, as difficult as it was for her, brought much healing for my own heart as I learned that I was dearly missed and loved when my mother had to let me go for a couple years.

Nevertheless, earlier in life, being separated from my parents also had quite a devastating impact on me. My safety, protection, peace, identity, and innocent childhood were all impacted by this deceptive stronghold of knowledge. It set me up for many levels of trauma, including me losing my parents for five of the most important years of my life. At four, I was also separated from my grandmother, who was the only source of love and security I knew up to that point in my life. As I've shared, I developed instability and insecurity issues. Dealing with these issues took years of healing my heart. My ability to communicate with my parents suffered in a devasting way for years after I was reunited with them at age six. The stronghold of knowledge was the underpinning of most of our conversations through much of my upbringing.

As I mentioned in the last chapter, most of our conversations were centered around performance, which was based on me developing knowledge. Instead of my parents starting with a relational question like, "How are you?" their questions would revolve around school. They would ask, "What are you studying? What tests do you have? How are your scores?" and so on. This dialogue is typical in almost every Indian household. Just like with performance, knowledge seemed to be more important than my emotional health. I don't blame the nature of our conversation on my parents, but I see it as a harmful effect from the idolatry of knowledge in my birth nation, which I will discuss more in the upcoming section, "Exposing the Stronghold."

FINDING MY FREEDOM

When I received my physical therapy degree and then landed my position as director of a physical therapy clinic, I was at a high level in my career, making an excellent salary. I achieved success, but I still felt inadequate. My parents encouraged me to continue my education to earn my doctorate. I chose not to because that was about that time that I realized that I had been idolizing knowledge and began to understand that I was bound by a stronghold. I knew that I had to break free.

I then understood that the first step to breaking free was acknowledging my need to break free.

I also recognized that I had been living on a hamster wheel; I had been spinning, hoping to be smart enough to be esteemed by my parents and my Asian Indian friends. When does this pursuit of knowing enough ever end unless you get off the hamster wheel? I knew that the way I was living did not leave me feeling content. Instead, I always wanted more.

I realized that the second step to freedom was changing my perception of my internal value and relearning how I would obtain that value.

As I thought about getting off this wheel, I had to count the cost. Would my parents or my Indian friends think that I was not as successful or as intelligent as other Indians? I realized that I could not spend the rest of my life caring about my family's and my friends' perception of me. I had to let go of my parents' expectations as well as my culture's expectation of who I should be and become comfortable with myself. I chose to no longer place my value on my level of my intelligence or on the degree or title I had by my name. This self-acceptance was the beginning of stepping into the new dreams ahead of me that I could not see before because I was blinded and burdened by the stronghold of knowledge.

As I've mentioned, the Asian Indian culture places little value on creativity or dreaming, as those things aren't considered academic pursuits. Creativity is a hobby to an Indian scholar.

I discovered that the third step to breaking free from the stronghold of knowledge is to begin to dream.

Dreaming and creating seemed like a foreign language to me because I did not value these activities until I got married in my mid-20s. My husband was such a dreamer and visionary; he could see things 20 years in the future. For me, however, the knowledge stronghold was buried so deep in my mind that even the word *creativity* used to make me cringe. The knowledge stronghold that had been at work actually minimized my creativity. As a result, I didn't try to be creative. I thought I wasn't good at being creative, and anything I thought I was not good at, I dismissed from my life.

This lack of creativity caused obstacles in my spiritual vision. When I drove into an inner-city community that had broken dreams and broken lives like the broken glass embedded in the ground, I could only see what was in front of me—brokenness. I had been trained all my life to only look at my reality. I remember the day my husband brought the idea to me that he was feeling called by God to serve the inner-city community. I was horrified—terrified, actually. Why? Because it was the unknown, and I could not creatively imagine the benefits of serving in the inner city. All I could see was what the media had painted the inner city be: murder, violence, prostitution, dog fights, drugs, and other problems. Don't get me wrong—these problems were real. Yet there was beauty in this community. I just couldn't see the hidden treasures amidst the extreme devastation that was so apparent. My previous lack of dreaming and practicing creativity had clouded my vision.

My husband, on the other hand, in spite of the difficulties, saw a canvas of dreams in this community, which he could see filled with hope and life. Through his leadership and example, I slowly began to see his dreams becoming reality in front of my eyes. He had consecrated his ideas to God. He had submitted his mind and knowledge to God. God's dreams about this community were being downloaded to my husband. I believe God gave my husband these dreams because of his submission to Him. I began to see that I too could be free to dream and have vision. I started to break free from the knowledge stronghold that had enslaved me for years. As I broke free, I was able to dream alongside my husband.

I could finally dream and see a future community rebuilt with love and purpose. I could see the poverty cycles restored by hope. I could see single moms equipped and empowered to raise their children with abundant life instead of them being trapped in the dysfunctional cycles of drug addiction, violence, and physical or emotional abuse.

I am reminded of the biblical definition of faith, which says "faith is being sure of what you hope for and certain of what you do not see" (Hebrews 11:1). The Bible also says, "without vision and hope, people perish" (Proverbs 29:18). Relying on knowledge and human capabilities alone in place of vision causes vision and dreams to die. My husband and I dreamt of rebuilding a community that was devastated with God's dreams, which were to transform one of the darkest places into a piece of Heaven on Earth.

My natural brain gravitated to logic and reason, so rebuilding this broken, devastated community did not compute in my mind at first. Why would I, being a newlywed, consider letting my husband dream of rebuilding the community when I could only think that doing so would lead to one of us being murdered? As I've mentioned, the media had already planted an extraordinary amount of fear inside of me because they only covered the violence in the area. What I learned in that season of my life is that fear drowns out faith. Lack of faith drowns out hope. But when faith is restored, hope can spring forth into life again. Faith allows us to see and trust God's promise and dreams for a people group beyond what is seen with the natural eye.

After dreaming, the next step I learned to break free was asking God to give me the gift of faith so that I could have hope—even in the midst of darkness.

This process is exactly what happened to my husband and me. Because of God's faithfulness, we developed hope beyond our understanding—at least, hope beyond my understanding. My husband seemed to have understanding from God and unswerving hope. Looking back on this situation, it is easy to see from a human perspective why I struggled with hope. The hope in this community seemed overshadowed by darkness.

To help you understand why darkness abounded in this area, I'll share with you a bit more about the community's history. In 1956, John Henry Hale, an inner-city Section 8 (government housing) project community had been given a prison sentence, and it was destined for hell. This part of the city, as I have mentioned, was often referred to as Hell's Half Acre. Why? Because African Americans were corralled into these government housing projects without help from the rest of fellow men, and at the same time, these communities were labeled dangerous. These labels were reinforced with generational, dysfunctional cycles of verbal abuse, sexual abuse, and drug addiction. Making matters worse was an epidemic

92

of fatherlessness both because of promiscuity and because additional government assistance was promised if mothers stayed single and had multiple children outside of the covenant of marriage.

In 2006, 50 years after its inception, this community was literally given hope through a $27 million grant called The Hope Grant. I found it interesting that this grant came in the community's jubilee year. Biblically, the jubilee year is the 50th year, when the land gets returned back to its original purpose and slaves who work on the land are also freed. In its jubilee year, literally, an enslaved mindset of hopelessness was broken off of this community. It was restored better than it began. Our dream, planted by God, which I never thought would come true in my lifetime, came to fruition that year. I knew that the grant was just the beginning; much more would happen after that.

I am also thrilled to say that through the years as I served this community, I have also been freed from slavery to the stronghold of knowledge; instead, I am filled with faith, hope, and dreams. My dreams enable me to envision something so magnificent coming in the future of our inner city in Nashville—I see the birthing of imagination, creativity, and art. I see master chefs and entrepreneurs. I imagine a renaissance center built in the John Henry Hale community that will allow African Americans to fully thrive and hit their marks, no longer bound by their past. We are called to dream with God and make these dreams reality, to design centers of hope and renaissance bursting with creativity and fruit in the most devastated, hopeless places.

My breakthrough from the knowledge stronghold gave me a fresh understanding of godly knowledge, which is far more powerful than human knowledge. The Bible says we need knowledge: We need to seek wisdom, learn continually, and invite God into our learning processes. We cannot out-reason God; He surpasses reason! God leads us into all understanding when we trust Him. Consider Daniel: the other wise men could not interpret King Nebuchadnezzar's dream. God gave Daniel godly wisdom, which comes from the heart of God, who is all-wise and all-knowing. This wisdom led to Daniel having knowledge far beyond his years, allowing him to have tremendous favor with the king. He prospered even when his people were in a land of captivity.

Just as Daniel prospered in what would have been thought of as a dangerous place, I began to become free in a "dangerous place." As I became free and began to share what I was learning with members of our church community, they also became free and began to prosper.

Generational Freedom of Knowledge—And Amazing Results

In addition to changing me and affecting our larger church community, my freedom from the stronghold of knowledge changed how I parented my children. I intentionally raised Emily, our oldest, and Daniel, our youngest, to love knowledge and learning, but I tried not to put pressure on them to make good grades. I no longer idolized knowledge, academia, or intelligence. I wanted education to be the exploration of knowledge, and my hope was that they would love learning. I also wanted them to grow; learning can foster growth because knowledge empowers us to get sharpened in fields of interest. When Emily was about a year old, I started teaching her how to read, but in a way that was fun with games, singing, and playing. This method of teaching worked; her favorite book she begged to read was the dictionary. She was talking in full sentences by the time she was 14 months old. She began reading small books by the time she was three years old. Emily told us that she was planning to go to Vanderbilt University at the age of five—an idea that came to her without coercion from either my husband or me.

Emily had such a love for learning—so much so that she learned several languages on her own, including Celtic, Norwegian, Spanish, and German. She not only explored writing, reading, math, and sciences, but also creative activities like art, dance, acting, crocheting, cooking, photography, song writing, poetry, piano, violin, art, and calligraphy.

As I got healed from the stronghold of knowledge, I encouraged Emily in her creativity. Emily excelled in school, from elementary through high school. I even homeschooled her for a period of time in middle school, which was controversial, especially for an Indian mom. I did not know any other Indian moms who homeschooled during this time. My parents questioned my judgement, especially because the middle school she would have attended designed a gifted program specifically for Emily. But I felt strongly that homeschooling was the right decision. This choice allowed me to bond with her in a deep way and to invest in her emotional health and spiritual health as I helped her develop intellectually and creatively. I homeschooled her from the beginning of fifth through the end of eighth grade, and then we applied for the highly accelerated International Baccalaureate (IB) program. For her to be accepted into this rigorous academic training program, she had to score high on the standardized tests and have an exceptional interview. I was honestly not sure how she was going to do compared to students who had been in the public school system. To our surprise, she was chosen to do the IB program. She really thrived in it. After her senior year, she graduated in the top one percent of her class—even with her IB/AP classes, which are considered the most difficult courses and therefore the hardest to earn the highest grade point average.

Emily succeeded in this accelerated environment, where she developed an amazing learning process because of a love for learning. I did my best to instill in her that knowledge comes from God. I also encouraged her to dream with God and to invite Him into the learning process. Scott and I didn't put any pressure on her to do anything. Instead, we went out of our way to make sure she knew that we loved her just as she was—not because of her intelligence.

When the time came for Emily to pick an undergraduate college, I believe all the years my husband and I spent pouring into the African American culture was beautifully reciprocated. Fisk University, a traditionally all African American school, granted Emily a full-ride undergraduate scholarship. Fisk had a very special accelerated bridge program, which enabled Emily to do one year at Fisk and two years at Vanderbilt to complete her undergraduate degree. Then came one of the most difficult parts of her education—picking where to do her graduate work to pursue her career. Emily wanted to fulfill her dream to bring health and healing to people. So, she chose to be a nurse practitioner. She decided on her own to apply to some of her favorite Ivy League schools: Vanderbilt, Yale, and Emory. She put in the application for the schools without my knowledge or consultation. In fact, I had suggested she apply to some state schools, since I did not want to put on her the unhealthy pressure that I received growing up.

Only after she had submitted her applications to her chosen schools did she inform me of her choices. I was so proud and amazed when she got accepted to her top three choices! Emily selected Vanderbilt out of all the universities because it had been her dream school since childhood. We rejoiced with her choice, but we started to wonder how we would pay for her tuition of almost $100,000 a year. If the tuition wasn't shocking enough, I got another shock: a couple days after Emily put her security deposit down for Vanderbilt's nurse practitioner program in faith God would provide, Emily received one of the largest merit scholarships Vanderbilt offered without even applying for it. God knew the desires of her heart, and He gifted her this scholarship to cover her higher education.

This unexpected scholarship showed me that fostering a love for learning in our children without pressuring them will make it more likely that they will NOT become bound by a stronghold of knowledge, but instead, they may even be rewarded because of the healthy knowledge they develop. Because I was no longer bound by the knowledge stronghold, I was able to break the generational and cultural pattern that valued intellect above everything else. Instead, I was able to foster and nourish our children's physical, emotional, and spiritual health. Focusing on these aspects of their lives freed them to excel in their intellectual capabilities on their own.

EXPOSING THE STRONGHOLD

This section will help you see the potential trap of the knowledge stronghold, both for yourself and for society at large.

Before I talk about the effects of the stronghold of knowledge, I want to say that I believe the saying that knowledge is power. However, I also believe knowledge without acknowledging the All-knowing One is foolishness. "Man's knowledge is futile" (Psalms 94:11). Just like knowledge is not bad, love of knowledge is also not bad, but when love of knowledge becomes idolatry because it is placed above God or is not submitted to God, that love of knowledge becomes problematic. The stronghold of knowledge exalts or makes an idol of man's intelligence by placing it above God's intelligence.

People with this stronghold set the highest value on academics, logic, reasoning, and revering the mind. These values may lead to an obsession, or even worship, of education and knowledge. For those bound in a knowledge stronghold, this worship of education and knowledge usurps the individual's relationship with God. This stronghold may also make that person prideful, self-governing, mistrusting of God, and independent.

Letting knowledge be exalted above a relationship with Father God can have devastating effects over time. This knowledge stronghold leads to unnecessary pain and devastation in an individual and in his or her family as well as in the generations to come. In the beginning, however, this stronghold can be covert. I would even suggest that if you aren't submitting your knowledge to God, the adversary, Satan, could be ruling the knowledge in your life.

STRONGHOLD THREE: KNOWLEDGE

We would all be wise to check ourselves to allow God to free us before this stronghold gets worse. To begin to see if you might be under the influence of the stronghold of knowledge, I invite you to ask yourself the following questions:

- Do you find that you are constantly thinking about learning more so that you can get ahead of everyone else?

- Do you find yourself trying to prove your intelligence to others so that they will see you as valuable?

- Are you devastated if you find out you were wrong about a subject matter that you were an expert on?

If you answered yes to these questions, you may be in bondage to this stronghold. You will have a chance to assess your life more fully and to use the tools to secure your freedom at the end of this chapter. First, however, I want you to see how widespread and devastating the effects of this stronghold are. I've found this information helps people realize that they are not alone—and you aren't either! If we all do our part to dismantle this stronghold, the entire world could change!

In India

Some may think that Asian Indians would put the highest weight on spiritual matters because a large percentage of them worship large number of gods. The Asian Indian mind, however, defaults to the obsession of knowledge and reasoning/education over spiritual ideas.

As I've mentioned, the first question Asian Indians ask others is what they do for a living because they are measuring the knowledge of others. According to the culture, the more knowledge a person has, the more honor is given to them. If I said I went to an Ivy League school, an Asian Indian would automatically set a high value on the amount of knowledge I have, and they would settle in their minds that I am capable and smart. This evaluation process puts a tremendous amount of pressure on children growing up, and for most, that pressure begins in pre-school. Children are judged and pressured every day from that early age based on intellect just as I was. This hidden knowledge stronghold has caused Indian parents to value their children's intellect or test scores more than the children's emotional health.

So much value is put on intellect, logic, and reasoning in India that creativity is not valued nearly as much as knowledge in Indian culture. Dancing, singing, painting, acting are all, in the Asian Indian brain, considered hobbies. If you do any of these activities as a career, you are judged and devalued—unless you are a top Bollywood actor or actress. In the Indian social class I was raised in, it is almost taboo to think about marrying someone with an artistic career. Therefore, in Indian culture, this stronghold has a significant effect on whom you marry. When parents pick the future marriage partners for their children, they put more value on the level of knowledge and education the potential partner has than on that person's personality and character. Don't get me wrong: people still put a high value on the character of the person, but education and intelligence most often take the leading role. Although I believe education and the gaining of knowledge is a privilege and not to be taken for granted, in an Asian Indian household, education, as I've said, is idolized. Just like the highest attainment for an entertainer is an industry award like an Oscar, or for an athlete, the highest achievement is going to the Olympics, the ultimate goal in Indian culture is an Ivy League education.

The Dangers of Humanism Worldwide

As I've alluded to, one of the biggest problems with the stronghold of knowledge is that it glorifies the mind, placing the utmost value on human intellectual capabilities. We as humans are not just a mind; we have a physical body. We have a soul, which is the mind, will, and emotions. We also have the spirit, which is the part that enables us to be connected to God if we choose to believe in Him. When we see knowledge as more important than tuning into the Holy Spirit, who lives within us and speaks truth, we are in danger of deception.

The human race is in danger of this deception because of the prevalence of humanism, which grows out of a stronghold of knowledge. Humanism has penetrated many spheres of influence, including education, government, arts and entertainment, as well as other areas. The most dangerous part of humanism is that it dismisses *ultimate truth, which comes from the Word of God,* especially in the area of morals or beliefs. In Genesis 3, God tells us that Eve took the fruit from the forbidden Tree of the Knowledge of Good and Evil because she wanted to gain wisdom and be like God. One characteristic of humanism, which the serpent used against Eve, is discrediting God's Word, and therefore His knowledge. Her desire to have knowledge above her relationship with God opened the door for evil to enter the world. In fact, there has been a war for whose knowledge we listen to since the time when Adam and Eve ate from that tree. When God is deleted from knowledge, however, truth is disintegrated.

In humanism, man defines morality. If a human does something that does not seem acceptable, it cannot be questioned because truth is relative to the individual. If man's truth opposes what the Bible says, it does not matter because there is no ultimate truth.

Therefore, humanism can be quite dangerous because it presents no plumbline for what is right or wrong.

Humanism is the worldview that makes it possible for people to call evil, "good" and good, "evil." Humanism makes it more plausible that evil will triumph, since people will be deceived into thinking that evil is actually good. The prophet Isaiah also says in Chapter 5 that some will swap darkness for light and light for darkness, and some will consider bitter to be sweet and sweet to be bitter. Culture has increasingly embraced humanism, which espouses ideas that flip truth, whether they are moral, pertaining to what is good or bad, or even biological, in the cases of gender, identity, and race.

When this characteristic of humanism plays out in a person's life, he or she engages in self-governing and becomes distrusting of authority. In more than 30 years of leading people through healing, I've learned most of the problematic issues are rooted in self-governance, which stems from a lack of protection from a parent of trusted figure. This perceived lack of protection creates distrust of any authority, and ultimately, rebellion. The idolatry of knowledge creates rebellion and autonomy from authority, disregarding divine order in favor of self-rule. This disregard for divine order fosters rebellion in the hearts of people, and rebellion leads to chaos and division.

We saw an example of humanism play out in what Hitler did exterminating the Jews. He called evil good (killing people). He also called the evil of being his own God good, because he thought he had the right to decide who was worthy to live or die. Hitler believed he could play with the gene pool in the way he wanted to in order to shape society to serve his empire-building interests.

Unfortunately, Hitler wasn't the only one trying to manipulate the minds of people. Bioengineering, also known as gene pool shaping, still goes on today. Scientists in genetic engineering are creating systems so that parents can select desirable traits in their offspring. Others are developing artificial intelligence to replace or program the free minds God gave to each of us. We are already beginning to see the potential dangers of substituting artificial intelligence for the minds God gave us with job elimination, societal manipulation, medical imposition, a lack of respect for individuals value, and a lack of mercy for difficult circumstances.

Although these societal situations are difficult, God is looking to break this stronghold, one person at a time. And through a collective group of free people banding together with His leadership, He will equip His people to fight these threats with His antidotes. Let's now take a look at what freedom from this stronghold might look like as we consider His invitation to break free to live free.

ESCAPING THE STRONGHOLD

This section is your invitation to break free so you can live free.

God is inviting us to engage in learning by acquiring knowledge inspired by His Word. When human knowledge is submitted and bound to the knowledge of God, then He can use our knowledge and expand it.

We can join God in learning as He directs us to and we can, in turn, invite God into our knowledge-seeking process. Then we can ask Him to deliver us from any stronghold of knowledge, just as I did! In other words, we can break free and live free—and dismantle this stronghold!

Breaking free creates the mental space for us to enjoy learning for the first time or for our passion to be reignited for learning. After we have broken free, both education and dreaming with God becomes exhilarating!

After we break free, intelligence levels do not define us anymore because our identity is not based on the level of education we have or on our intelligence. Our creative minds and imaginations, as well as our ability to reason and use logic, are gifts we celebrate. Each of us can live a life based on THE truth in God's Word instead of living out of our own truth. Our knowledge is not limited because we are partnering with All-knowing One.

When we dream, we can create things and bring them into reality. We were designed to co-create with God. When we dream and begin to take steps toward those dreams, we tap into the Creator, who establishes all things, and since we are created in His image, our creativity flows. Knowledge consecrated to God allows creativity to flow because He is the master creator of design and knowledge. We become able to remove the limits from our dreams, and we begin to dream God's big dreams for ourselves, which frees us to walk out supernaturally infused lives.

Breaking a stronghold as we have learned begins with identifying a problem and then repenting. The fruit of repentance is change and transformation.

I invite you to take the first step out of the bondage of the knowledge stronghold. Over time, as you move forward, you too will experience breakthrough—you will receive new freedom. Instead of relying on your own mind for wisdom, you will gain powerful wisdom from His truth. You will have an avid love for learning, and you will dream big, God-sized dreams.

Are you ready to take the first step to getting free from the stronghold of knowledge?

As I've mentioned, the first step to breaking free is self-awareness. Examine the list in the next section to see if you have this stronghold of knowledge operating in your life. If you are experiencing the negative effects of the stronghold of knowledge, you will identify with some of these statements.

ASSESSING YOURSELF

Knowledge Mindset Identifiers

For each stronghold, there are 20 identifiers listed. As you read, put a check mark by the ones you feel apply to you. Each check mark will be considered one point. Add up the check marks, which will give you the total points for this stronghold. By the end of this book, you will be able to rank which stronghold needs the most attention first by the greatest number of points. (Most people have some of each; if this happens to you, don't be discouraged. God will enable you to break free of every stronghold—it just may take some time.)

1. I tend to derive my value from my level of education.
2. I tend to derive value from being more intelligent than others.
3. I get value from having a better education than others.
4. I get value based on the university or school I attended.
5. I tend to feel strong pressure to perform.
6. I tend to be unusually competitive.
7. I tend to constantly compare myself to others.
8. My love for learning and natural curiosity has dwindled.
9. I tend to have trouble with believing the ultimate truth of God's Word.
10. I tend to put logic over faith.
11. I tend to dislike creativity.
12. I have a hard time dreaming/I dislike dreamers.
13. I have a hard time connecting with God because He doesn't fit into the box of reason.
14. I tend to devalue people who are less intelligent.
15. I tend to dismiss the supernatural.

16. I tend to believe my intelligence is equal to or superior to God.

17. I focus on academics in my children without considering their emotional health or their creative gifts like singing, dancing, art, poetry, photography.

18. I tend to live my life based on my own definition of truth.

19. I feel shame or embarrassment when comparing myself to more intelligent people.

20. I believe I can live my life without God's input.

Reflection Questions

Take a few moments to get quiet and think about the following reflection questions and write your answers in a journal.

1. Have you personally encountered the knowledge stronghold in your life? How did it negatively affect you?

2. What symptoms of the knowledge stronghold have you noticed in your life?

3. Was there a part of my story that you related to in your own life?

4. On a scale of 0-10 how would you rate this stronghold affecting your life?

5. What are two action steps you can put in place to activate a love for learning without idolizing knowledge?

STEPPING INTO YOUR FREEDOM!

If you recognize this knowledge stronghold in yourself, then use the following steps to break free of this stronghold's constraints, which have hindered your maximum potential. I want you to live free to break free!

Repent

Pray with me:

"God, I'm so sorry. As Your child, I'm so sorry for every way I partnered with the knowledge stronghold and allowed the stronghold to rule my life, decisions, and thinking patterns. Your Word says to take every thought captive to the obedience of Christ, and I am taking this stronghold of knowledge captive! The knowledge stronghold is no longer allowed to confine me."

Renounce

To renounce a stronghold is to break agreement with toxic beliefs that have formed a stronghold. When we renounce something, we make a declaration that we no longer affiliate with that system of beliefs.

Break agreements with the following statements that apply to you. I break agreement with the stronghold of knowledge because:

- I have seen myself as intellectually superior to others.
- I have felt shame when I compare my intellect to others.
- I have controlled and manipulated others using my intellect.
- I have embraced worldly knowledge based in humanism.
- I have derived my value from my IQ and from my education. performance in school or in college.

- I have thought that using imagination, dreaming, and being creative is foolish or unnecessary.
- I have been self-reliant in acquiring knowledge and wisdom.
- I have lived life based on my own definition of truth.
- I have believed that my Intelligence is superior to God.
- I have been harshly critical of myself or others.

Declare with me:

"I renounce and break all agreements I have made with the stronghold of knowledge. Specifically, I renounce the beliefs of worldly knowledge found in the statements I just broke agreement with. I am so sorry, God, for coming into agreement with the stronghold of knowledge, and I am sorry for how I have lived my life based on the effects of the stronghold of knowledge. Please forgive me, Father God, for living my life not consecrating this gift of knowledge to You so that You could make it flourish and create innovative ideas that would help the world around me."

Release

Pray with me:

"Father God, I release this knowledge stronghold and place it at Your feet. Break me free from all the ways this knowledge stronghold has affected my life and those around me, including unnecessary shame as I compared my intellect to others like my peers, classmates, or siblings. I also release any thoughts of seeing myself as intellectually superior to others. I receive the power of Your blood to wash and renew me. Today I choose to fully receive You and to live my life consecrating my mind and knowledge to You."

Restore

Pray with me:

"God, what do you want to give me in place of the stronghold of knowledge?"

Listen carefully and journal what He speaks to you. When you let go of something that was not healthy or good, God always replaces it with good things. So, thank God for this good gift and walk out your life with it.

Rewire

Say with me:

- *"I am deeply loved by God, and this divine love is not based on my IQ, education, performance in school, work, or interests.*
- *I am blessed and walking in all the gifts that God wants to activate in me as I consecrate the gift to learn, understand, and seek knowledge to Him. I am an active learner.*
- *I am walking in the fulfillment of every promise God has for my life.*
- *I am overturning the demonic tactics that the enemy has put in my life through the stronghold of knowledge. I am walking out of every trap that has been set for me.*
- *I am unraveling the effects of the stronghold of knowledge in my life and family bloodline.*
- *I am accessing my God-given inheritance as I activate the gift of knowledge and use it to dream God's dreams for my life.*
- *I am receiving revelation and wisdom to bring breakthroughs in all spheres of society I am to influence (pick which sphere applies*

to you) such as education, entertainment, media, religion, business, government, etc."

Scriptures to Meditate on

- Isaiah 11:2—The Spirit of the LORD will rest on him—

  the Spirit of wisdom and understanding

  the Spirit of counsel and might,

  the Spirit of the knowledge and fear of the LORD.

- James 1:5 (ESV)—If any of you lacks wisdom, let him ask God, who give generously to all without reproach, and it will be given him.

- Proverbs 2:6—For the LORD gives wisdom, from his mouth comes knowledge and understanding.

- 2 Corinthians 10:5—We demolish arguments and every pretension that sets itself up against the knowledge of God, and we take captive every thought to make it obedient to Christ.

- Proverbs 20:24—A person's steps are directed by the LORD. How then can anyone understand their own way?

- John 17:17—Sanctify them by the truth; your word is truth.

- Genesis 3:4–5—The serpent said to the woman, "You surely will not die! "For God knows that in the day you eat from it your eyes will be opened, and you will be like God, knowing good and evil."

Closing Prayer

"Father, by the power and authority You have, would You rebuke and dismantle the stronghold of knowledge from my life. I ask that this stronghold of knowledge would not bear fruit ever again in me. God, with Your angelic armies, strip the power from this knowledge stronghold and free me from its grip. Lord of Hosts, I invite You to remove and uproot any way the stronghold of knowledge has tormented my life as well as the lives of my family. Father God, carry this stronghold of knowledge out now. This stronghold will go to the place Jesus sends it, and never return, in the name of Jesus Christ of Nazareth. Father I give you permission to rewire my brain and change my thinking concerning this stronghold of knowledge. Your Word says that if anyone lacks wisdom, ask and You will give it generously. Therefore, I shall have wisdom. I apply the blood of Jesus over my mind, and I have the mind of Christ; I have his thoughts. In Jesus' name I pray! Amen."

MAMMON

"Not he who has much is rich, but he who gives much."[6]*—Eric Fromm*

MY STORY

At 25 years old, I had reached many of my goals; I was primed to take on the world. I graduated from a wonderful university program, and I was ready to "climb the corporate ladder," even though I was in the physical therapy field. I wanted to make as much money as I could to show my family, friends, and society that I was a successful and prosperous woman. There was only one mountain of my young life left to conquer: marriage. I knew that I could drive a deeper stake into the ground by making a strong choice for a life partner. I had learned that the ideal spouse was a wealthy spouse. You see, every Indian parent's dream is to have a son or daughter marry into money. That is why, in an arranged marriage, there is just as much weight put on the type of career and therefore money the future mate will have as the character of the person who is being considered. The fixation on a person's financial status is evidence of a stronghold of mammon operating in Indian culture, which I'll talk about more in the section, "Exposing the Stronghold." Before I share how I ended up with a pastor instead of a person of higher financial means, let me define the stronghold of mammon, and relay how it had gripped my life.

Mammon is the idolatry of money or riches. Mammon is an Aramaic word that means *riches*, and it comes from the Syrian God of riches, known by the same name. Jesus said that one cannot serve both God and Mammon. Enjoying money is not evil, but the love of money becomes idolatry when wealth holds greater trust and affection than God. That kind of idolatry then gives root to the stronghold of mammon. **This stronghold operates on people who do not submit their money to God.**

As a young person, I loved money. If it was $100 or $1,000, no matter what amount, I loved counting it. Sometimes I would count it over and over again. I loved the feel of having money in my hands. Maybe you could say I was obsessed with money. When I got a paycheck, I would go to the bank, cash my check, and then come home and count my money. I was fixated on making money, keeping it, and multiplying it. I was not a generous person (I did not have this realization until I met my husband, who is tremendously generous). I always looked for the best deals so I would not have to spend much money. I felt a tremendous amount of pressure to be successful, to make as much money as I could, and to marry someone with equal financial ambitions.

I can remember the strain on my emotions when my husband wanted to give well above and beyond the limits I had set in my mind as a donation to a ministry. I was shocked at the idea, and it hurt me to stretch my faith like that. Giving, however, was another step to breaking the power of the mammon stronghold in my life.

114

Maybe you are not as obsessed as I was, counting every dollar and fixating on your income. I believe, however, that most people have experienced the anxiety of financial pressure, the fear of lack, or the pride of monetary security at least at some point, if not often, in their lives.

Growing up, I desperately wanted my parents' approval. As I've shared, when I was old enough to marry, I went to my parents and asked them to work on arranging (or setting up) my marriage. I wanted to have their approval on whom I would marry. In the process of an arranged marriage in the Indian culture, the parents gather information and data from all around the world of potential suitors to find the right fit for their daughter or son. Included in this information are biographies from the suitors with information on family background, education, religious background, and the most important factor, their chosen profession, which is used to project and discern their financial status. I think my parents had this process down to a science because of how many times they had to find new suitors—I was quite particular. Each time I said no to one of the men they would bring, they had to find another one just as suitable with similar criteria in each of the categories I mentioned above. In this arranged marriage process, you have only one day to meet the possible suitor and ask questions and get to know him. At the end of the day, I had to make a decision to marry him or not. I had to tell many of the suitors that my parents brought that they were not the right match for me.

One day my parents set me up with an electrical engineer who was also a theologian. He was a great public communicator, tall, good-looking, fair complexion, but most of all, he was successful in his professional career and made quite a bit of money. As far as arranged marriages go, this was the best scenario! On paper, he seemed like the perfect match. He had a few negative character traits that I dismissed because I so wanted to please my parents and go along with their arrangement. God, however, was about to preset a different arrangement, that if I agreed, would alter the course of every aspect of my life.

FINDING MY FREEDOM

One week from finalizing this arranged marriage is when I met Scott, who loved Jesus and had a great personality. Scott was about six feet tall with brown hair and eyes that glowed when he talked about Jesus. He was a Christian music producer. In an Indian parent's mind, being a Christian musician or producer is not a profession; it is a hobby. But through much prayer and many signs, God made it very clear to me that He wanted to arrange my marriage instead of my parents. Our love story is so special, but how we fell in love and what God did isn't the point of this section.

After I received supernatural signs that God was putting us together, I was then faced with a difficult decision: If I chose the man I had been arranged to be married to, I would be financially secure for life. If I chose Scott, I would be marrying someone because of his love for Jesus, but I would have little assurance of financial security. Many people do not realize how much they love money, but I did. I cannot lie: I loved material things. I loved having the best clothes, the best shoes, the best handbags. I built my whole life with a mindset to make it to the top of the ladder of success and to make as much money as I could so I would be successful and also look successful. I had dreams of having servants like I did in childhood. The reality was setting in that I could lose perceived financial peace, happiness, and security if I did not pick mammon— which would bring everything money could buy. Before me was black-and-white choice to choose the love of money or the love for the Kingdom of God. The decision felt like jumping out of an airplane, freefalling into the unknown. I was scared, but I knew I had an opportunity for freedom. With this one brave choice, I could break out of thousands of years of family and cultural tradition.

I have realized in my life that every small decision aligned with God affects not just our own lives, but it ripples through the generations, writing a much larger storyline than we know. Incredibly, the man with whom I was supposed to be arranged with had the last name of Mammon! Scott's last name is MacLeod, which means "Hold Fast." 1 Thessalonians 5:21 says to examine everything carefully and HOLD FAST to what is good. Now we say, "Hold fast to the Lord." Scott is so passionate about this message that he also includes this line under every email or letter he sends.

After many tears and prayers, and counting the cost, I made the decision! I chose that day to pick Scott MacLeod. I chose to *hold fast* in faith to what is good. That day, the one decision was the beginning of breaking out of the unhealthy love of money stronghold. When I made that choice, I knew that I was directly going against everything I had known and been taught. I was choosing a life of simplicity and investing in something that money can't buy—people. I was finally living by faith and trusting God to be my provider. I was free from idolizing money.

When I chose to go with God's arrangement for my marriage, I knew that I was intentionally surrendering my love for money to choose a love for the Kingdom of God. I was storing my treasures in Heaven, not storing the treasures here on earth. Breaking the love of money and being fixated on it began the process of getting free from the stronghold of mammon, which had been suffocating my life. My freedom also affected my family's lives moving forward.

Honestly, I had never acknowledged God concerning money. I always thought we work hard, earn it, and use it for whatever we want. The concept that God is our provider and wants to provide for us was foreign to me. I thought I was the financial provider by getting educated, working hard, and earning money. I had been taught that God provided the brains so that I can make the money.

I remember when Scott was renovating our first building to start our ministry serving in the inner city. It was an old historic building built in the early 1900s, and we needed a considerable amount of money for the renovation. I honestly did not understand what he was saying. I said, "Why do you ask God for money when you can make money yourself? Why don't I just work for three or four years, and then we will get enough money and fix this building?" Scott reassured me and said, "If God has told us to renovate this building to start serving the poor, He will help provide the finances." This assertion did not make any sense in my logical brain, so I let it go and let Scott figure out how to renovate that building. For every part of the building, Scott would ask God to provide, and I watched God provide. One of the first parts of renovation we needed to build was our cafe ´. Shortly after Scott prayed, God provided through a mall being torn down and the owner donating all the doors and windows from that mall. These materials were precisely what we needed to build the café. Next, we needed air-conditioning. The old building needed brand new duct work, which cost tens of thousands of dollars. Scott prayed, and God provided and sent an air-conditioning company that performed all the labor completely free. This story was the first of thousands where God provided for us…I realized that God delights in being our provider!

The Path of Servanthood and Generosity

As the stronghold of mammon continued to be dismantled in my life, I started to break free from the endless pursuit of upward mobility. Instead, I deliberately chose a path of servanthood and generosity. Through the years, God has given Scott and I the privilege of sowing financially into underserved communities in our own city as well as worldwide. Did we do it all perfectly? Absolutely not! We did not know what we were doing in the beginning, but we had hearts willing and set on living a minimalist lifestyle so that we could generously give of our lives, money, and time.

Servanthood and the gift of generosity are keys to break the back of mammon. We decided to serve those who were destined for destruction by hopelessness, drugs, violence, prostitution—generational cycles that became shackles of pain, anxiety, and fear. People were trapped without intervention. Scott and I both gave up our successful career paths: music for Scott and medicine for me. Our goals became to bind up the pain of the brokenhearted, set captives free, and preach the good news to the poor.

Not only did God help me develop the first key, generosity, through money, but He developed generosity in my time, my talents, and my life in general. The other key to break mammon is to serve people who can never repay you. This act cleanses our hearts from underlying selfish motives, with which we serve someone to receive something in return. Were our generous and servant-hearted efforts worth it? Absolutely yes! *We have watched a community of about 4,000 single moms, drug dealers, and broken children being infused with hope, life, and a future!*

We cannot give to someone or something that we have not received or walked out in our own lives. When the cycle of the stronghold of money is broken off of an individual by generosity and consecrated giving, that breakthrough releases spiritual authority for the cycle of poverty to be broken off an entire region. Just as my "no" to Mr. Mammon and my "yes" to Mr. "Hold Fast" broke the stronghold of money over my life, it also made the way for me to say yes to God's generosity. That decision invited me to be part of breaking the vicious cycle of poverty and lack over a devastated community. If I had not escaped out of my generational dysfunctional patterns caused by the idolatry of mammon, I would not have seen the actual needs of this community, which was filled with the fear of lack and bound in poverty cycles. If I had chosen to continue in my self-serving ways and the ways of the ancient traditions of the culture of my birth country, I would have continued to live for my bank account and for the prestige of earthly treasures. I would have missed out on the blessings of something much greater than trying to preserve my own life and possessions.

The gift of generosity allows us to sow into individuals, people groups, and regions. Generosity brings restoration, which results in transformation. This transformation is exactly what happened in our John Henry Hale community. I was able to break free, which gave me the tools and resources to help open up abundant provision for our inner-city families and culture to thrive! We have generously sown into this community to give it life and hope, not just with money, but with time, energy, God's Word, and discipleship of the people—especially the children. Our goal was to give them a legacy of hope for their future. I could have never imagined the impact this one decision of coming out of the stronghold of mammon and marrying Scott would make in my life and in the lives of so many.

We have poured into more than 1.5 million lives in our city and in 25 nations around the world since 1993. This number seems unbelievable looking back on it! I've been asked as to how we have served so many. Some of these efforts I have already mentioned, including weekly church services, food and clothing distribution outreaches, Bible studies, and dance workshops. I'll also highlight some of our other efforts to help you get an understanding of the type of work God has blessed us to be a part of. We minister to around 1,000 people a week on Nashville's Broadway, the touristy, well-known street in the heart of downtown, where many of the bars are with live music. We also have young adult worship nights, camps, and a ministry school. We have hosted community and friendship building gatherings though the years with pastors. We have prison outreach and nursing home outreach. We have sent teams overseas to serve communities in 25 nations and we have also gone to 12 Native American reservations. In addition, we put on or are a part of conferences locally, nationally, and internationally. How is all of this possible? It is possible because we follow God's direction, serving where He sends us. We have seen miracle after miracle!

I believe my rejection of the love of money allowed me to be part of the biggest miracle—seeing our entire inner-city community transformed! Drugs, violence, and prostitution no longer control this area. I believe God wants to do this kind of marvelous transformation worldwide in many communities and nations. But this transformation cannot happen if people remain under the grip of mammon, which keeps its slaves in bonds of perpetual selfishness. It's time to serve the God of Mercy and not the god of money!

EXPOSING THE STRONGHOLD

This section will help you see the potential trap of the mammon stronghold, both for yourself and for society at large.

As I've mentioned, the stronghold of mammon is when people love money so much that they disregard God and His instructions of how to handle money in a godly way. Money itself is not evil; money is neutral. Loving and serving mammon is the root of all evil. This love of money is evident in the story of the rich young ruler in the Bible. This young man loved God, but he could not give up his possessions to follow Jesus. In the same way, our dependence on money, or mammon, becomes a stronghold in our lives when money is the foundation of our security instead of God.

People under the stronghold of mammon tend to make decisions based on their love of money instead of based on their God-given talents and purposes. They may also prioritize money over close relationships, and they may avoid connection with people who also don't love money. They may also think of themselves as superior to those who aren't as well-off as they are.

Some of you may be thinking: *We do not need to worry about this stronghold operating in our lives because we don't have much money.* In response to that thought, I have to say: This unhealthy mindset may be at work no matter how much money we have.

I invite you to begin to consider whether you may be under a stronghold of mammon. Have you:

1. Chosen a long-term career that doesn't suit your personality because of money?

2. Gotten into a romantic relationship or married someone who wasn't compatible with you because of a desire for money or to live "the good life?"

3. Not been in community with those who aren't as well off as you are?
4. Formed an opinion about the worth of an individual who isn't in the same socioeconomic class as you are?

If you answered yes to these questions, you may be in bondage to this stronghold. You will have a chance to more fully assess your life and to use the tools to secure your freedom at the end of this chapter. First, however, I want you to see how widespread and devastating the effects of this stronghold are. I've found this information helps people realize that they are not alone—and you aren't either! If we all do our part to dismantle this stronghold, the entire world could change!

The Impact of the Mammon Stronghold on India

As much as I love my birth country and my people, this ugly, all-consuming, pervasive stronghold of mammon has been at work there for centuries. Even though the idolatry of money exists throughout the world, it underpins many aspects of Indian society. Indians are prepared from childhood to seek the highest-ranking jobs, which bring power, status, and wealth. This mindset is ingrained in most Indian children, but I do not know that anyone intentionally says this is the goal out loud. As I've shared in other parts of this book, most Indians are taught from an early age to put an unusual value and trust in money because of the caste system that has its foundation in the Hindu religion, the major religion of the nation. Even if you are raised as a Muslim or Christian in India, the cultural mindset of the caste system affects the entire country. For thousands of years, the wealthy have privilege and honor as the highest caste, while the poor are dishonored and shamed in the lowest caste. This oppressive system causes even the poorest family to be under this mammon stronghold because parents do not want their children to be dishonored or shamed.

Sadly, because of the Hindu caste system, the rich stay rich and the poor stay poor. These beliefs cause an unhealthy fear of poverty, which drives the stronghold of mammon. The wealthy in the top caste, known as Brahmin, have servants and avoid jobs they do not want. They have most of the power in society, and because the Hindu belief claims they have earned their status, they are highly respected. The lowest caste, known as Dalits or "oppressed," must take the lowliest lots in society and, because their status is thought to be earned as well, they are degraded. In my opinion, the mammon stronghold is one of the most dominant in Indian culture. It has been ruling lives and generations for centuries, and it is a focal point of many Asian Indian lives.

As was the case with my own life, this mammon stronghold takes root in childhood. Questions about how a child is raised, educated, and who he or she eventually marries all center around money. There is tremendous pressure to be successful and educated if you do not want to be looked down on and end up on the streets cleaning sewers. If you are educated well, you will have a greater chance to have money, security, and status.

Fear of poverty even causes people to avoid charity and generosity. Many are enslaved by their fear of not having enough. This stronghold is at work, causing many Asian Indians to miss out on the numerous blessings of generosity in their lives. I believe as Asian Indians recognize and uproot this mammon stronghold out of their lives, they will no longer be bound and ensnared by it, and instead they will become some of the most generous people on

Earth. Instead of being consumed with personal financial security, they will be consumed with worldwide charity.

In addition to losing the blessing of generosity, many Indians may miss the blessings of individuality because of the stronghold of mammon. Children are discouraged from pursuits which may not earn a high income, such as athletics, artistry, or humanities. Each child, as we know, is blessed by God with unique talents, skills, and passions. But, as I've shared elsewhere, because of the focus on money, Indian children are pushed into university and career tracks based solely on potential earnings and the security that job can bring. Other interests are devalued as hobbies or leisure activities.

In addition to controlling careers, the mammon stronghold also influences marriages in Indian culture. Marriages are arranged by parents with behaviors that seem more like job interviews and contract negotiations than courtship. The marriage is viewed as a partnership based on economic potential whereby a person can achieve or maintain a high social status and security.

These negative aspects of the mammon stronghold on Indian culture are heavy and tangled, but Asians are not the only ones to be affected by this worship of money. As we will see, the roots of the love of money stretch far and wide.

The Mammon Stronghold in the U.S.

The stronghold of mammon is at work in our welfare system of government in the United States. People in the US stay in a poverty mentality and live dependent on the system. Welfare is not fair. It keeps people living and depending on a certain level of income. People feel that they never have enough, but they are deceived, thinking that they cannot survive without handouts from man-made institutions. This mammon stronghold continues to operate in our lives when we do not submit how we use our money to God.

A stronghold of mammon, as we have seen, operates in those people and systems who don't submit their money to God. This stronghold has a voice, and it speaks loudly! Its desire is to rule the hearts of men, and its siren calls can be hypnotizing. This enticing call is why many world leaders, CEOs of large corporations, and nations' leaders roll out the red carpet for money to take front and center. Money drives many industries including oil, cosmetics, candy, information systems, internet, sports, entertainment, retail, communications, and more—often to the detriment of humanity and morality. The Father gave us instructions and strategies on how to identify the stronghold of mammon and defeat it so it would not destroy us. I will share some of the specific places that God tells us how to deal with money in the section entitled, "Scriptures to Meditate on."

In *The Lord of the Rings* story, whoever holds the ring rules the world. Likewise, in our world, whoever holds the wealth holds the power. From my perspective, a worldwide war for wealth is raging because wealth leads to power. But the power given by mammon is false and temporary; the stronghold of mammon leads to perpetual enslavement.

ESCAPING THE STRONGHOLD

This section is your invitation to break free so you can live free.

I believe there are millions of people throughout the world who have the God-given gift of acquiring wealth and stewarding wealth, and they will no longer use it for selfish gain or power. Instead, they will use the finances, resources, and money for Kingdom investments. The return on this will be bountiful! Proverbs 3:9–10 reminds us that when we honor the Lord with our wealth and with the first fruits of all our produce, our barns will be filled with plenty.

The fastest way to break free from the control of mammon is to give thanks for the finances we receive and then consecrate these finances back to God. This consecration takes money out of the world's system and put it into God's hands. The practical steps of this process, according to scripture, include giving the first 10% to the house of God and then allowing God to redeem the rest of the money from the spirit of the world. He who is faithful with little is given much, so it is important that you consecrate the money back to God and thank Him for it. Then ask God how to multiply it.

How we handle, steward, and manage what we have is key. Wise handling and stewarding of money is taking good care of what we have by not overextending ourselves financially by purchasing unnecessary things. Overspending beyond our means keeps us enslaved to money. However, if we spend beneath our means, we will be able to walk toward financial freedom. Hopefully from my story, you can see that breaking free from mammon so that it doesn't sabotage your life is possible!

I believe that as you break out of the grip and enslavement of mammon, you are going to receive not only a breakthrough for yourself but also a breakthrough for your families and communities.

I can already see a ripple effect as whole areas previously destined for destruction come out from the grip of mammon. These communities will enter into their original design, exuding how they were created by the Creator. The people in these communities will live their lives to the fullest, counting their blessings—not what they don't have. They will use what God has put in their hands, instead of waiting for a handout.

I want to invite you to invest your resources to impact and transform the world. Compassionate generosity and kingdom investments are a blessing for others and a breakthrough for you. I want to help redirect your earthly treasure toward eternal Kingdom investments in ways that I've mentioned in this chapter.

If you recognize this mammon stronghold mindset is in you, then I invite you to use the steps in the next section to break free.

ASSESSING YOURSELF

Stronghold of Mammon Identifiers

For each stronghold, there are 20 identifiers listed. As you read, put a check mark by the ones you feel apply to you. Each check mark will be considered one point. Add up the check marks, which will give you the total points for this stronghold. By the end of this book, you will be able to rank which stronghold needs the most attention first by the greatest number of points. (Most people have some of each; if this happens to you, don't be discouraged. God will enable you to break free of every stronghold—it just may take some time.)

1. I tend to struggle with being generous with my money.
2. I tend to get anxious about not having enough money even when I'm making sufficient money.
3. I tend to struggle with feeling that I could become poor if I don't work hard enough.
4. I tend to grow jealous and envious when I see others prospering financially.
5. I tend to hesitate trusting God with my money.
6. I tend to believe that I would rather control my life and destiny than surrender my outcome to the Lord.
7. I tend to put much pressure on myself to be successful in my career.
8. I tend to consider my future mate based on how much money he makes instead of his character.
9. I tend to judge the poor, saying to myself, "They just need to get a job."
10. I tend to believe that I have worked hard for the money I earned, so I can do whatever I want with it.
11. I tend to only buy designer clothes, handbags, belts, shoes, etc.

12. I tend to spend much of my time seeing how much money I can save (even to the point of being called "Scrooge" or stingy).

13. I tend to be selfish and buy things for myself because I think I deserve it.

14. I tend to believe that my success and my identity as a person is dependent on how much money I make.

15. I tend to believe that tithing (giving 10%) of my income to my home church is unnecessary, and in general, I have hard time giving money joyfully.

16. I tend to believe that it is better to save money than enjoy it by spending it.

17. I tend to hoard things in my home in case I need them at some point.

18. I tend to base my security based on how much money is in my bank account and assets like my home, land, cars etc.

19. I tend to accumulate debt and solicit help from others to eliminate it rather than deal with it myself.

20. I tend to have more credit cards than I need.

Reflection Questions

Take a few moments to get quiet and think about the following reflection questions and write your answers in a journal.

1. Have you personally encountered the mammon stronghold in your life? How did it negatively affect you?

2. What symptoms of the mammon stronghold have you noticed in your life?

3. Was there a part of my story that you related to in your own life?

4. On a scale of 0–10, how would you rate your level of generosity? (0 is no generosity 10 is the best you can possibly do).

5. What are two action steps you can put in your life to be a kingdom investor?

Here are a few ideas about how you could become a Kingdom investor:

- Search in your city for missions or missionaries being equipped or find out where the impoverished part of the city is being served and invest money, time, and your resources there.

- Search in your city for a non-profit organization that offers a ministry/discipleship program for young adults in the inner city, in trailer parks, or in an underserved area.

- Search for land that a ministry is developing to build a mission base or to train missionaries.

- Sow into ministry training schools so that the next generation can get equipped and have resources.

STEPPING INTO YOUR FREEDOM

Repent

Pray with me:

"God, I'm so sorry. I repent for every way I have partnered with the mammon stronghold and allowed the stronghold to rule my life, decisions, and thinking patterns. Your Word says to take every thought captive to the obedience of Christ, and I am taking this stronghold of mammon captive! The mammon stronghold is no longer allowed to confine me or hold me captive."

Renounce

To renounce a stronghold is to break agreement with toxic beliefs that have formed a stronghold. When we renounce something, we make a declaration that we no longer affiliate with that system of beliefs.

Break agreements with the following statements that apply to you. I break agreement with mammon because:

- I have held my trust and affection for wealth over God, and money has been the foundation of my security instead of God.

- I have controlled career choices instead of asking God for His plan for my life.

- I have lacked generosity, and I have not modeled a generous lifestyle.

- I have feared lack (not having enough).

- I have relied on money to bring me security instead of trusting in God.

- I have overspent instead of living within my means.

- I have practiced hoarding out of fear of not having enough material things.
- I have been overdriven in an effort to get more money.
- I have feared poverty.
- I have only been giving to those who can pay me back.

Declare with me:

"I renounce and break all agreements I have made with the stronghold of mammon. Specifically, I renounce the beliefs of Mammon found in the statements above that I have just broken agreement with. I am so sorry, God, for coming into agreement with the stronghold of mammon and for how I have lived my life based on the effects of this stronghold. Please forgive me, Father God, for not modeling a generous lifestyle and for not consecrating my money to You. My desire is that You multiply the money You give to me so that I can use it as a blessing for others."

Release

Pray with me:

"Father God, I release this mammon stronghold and place it at Your feet. Break me free from all the ways this stronghold has affected my life and those around me, including making life decisions such as picking a career path or future mate based on this mammon stronghold, I am sorry; please forgive me. Today I choose to fully receive You and live my life consecrating my money to You. I receive the power of Your blood to wash and renew me."

Restore

Pray with me:

"God, what do You want to give me in place of the stronghold of mammon?"

Listen carefully and journal what He speaks to you or shows you. When you let go of something that was not healthy or good, God always replaces it with good things. So, thank God for this good gift, receive it freely, and walk it out daily in your life.

Rewire

The last step is restructuring our thinking patterns using the Word of God. Ask the Lord to show you His ways using scriptures. A few are listed in the next section to get you started. Remember to daily read these truths over yourself for at least the next 60 days so that it becomes a natural part of what you believe and therefore rewires your brain.

Say with me:

- *"I am deeply loved by God, and Your divine love isn't based on the type of career I have or the amount of money I make. Nor is Your love based on what family line I come from.*

- *I am blessed and walking in all the gifts that God wants to activate in me as I consecrate the gift of making money to Him. I live in the fulfillment of every promise God has for my life.*

- *I am overturning the demonic tactics that the enemy has put in my life through the stronghold of mammon. I am walking out of every trap that has been set for me.*

- *I am unraveling the effects of mammon in my life and family bloodline.*

- *I am receiving the fullness of my rich inheritance in Christ, and I am using my wealth to prosper the areas of health care, education, entertainment, religion, government, and (add your own areas of influence)."*

Scriptures to Meditate on

- Hebrews 13:5 (ESV)—Keep your lives free from the love of money and be content with what you have, because God has said, "I will never leave you nor forsake you."

- Mathew 6:26 (ESV)—Look at the birds of the air; they do not sow or reap or store away in barns, and yet your heavenly Father feeds them. Are you not much more valuable than they?

- 1 Chronicles 29:12—Wealth and honor come from you; you are the ruler of all things. In your hands are strength and power to exalt and give strength to all.

- Philippians 4:19—And my God will meet all your needs according to the riches of his glory in Christ Jesus.

- Luke 14:12–14—Then Jesus said to his host, "When you give a luncheon or dinner, do not invite your friends, your brothers or sisters, your relatives, or your rich neighbors; if you do, they may invite you back and so you will be repaid. But when you give a banquet, invite the poor, the crippled, the lame, the blind, and you will be blessed. Although they cannot repay you, you will be repaid at the resurrection of the righteous."

- Matthew 7:7—"Ask and it will be given to you; seek and you will find; knock and the door will be opened to you."

- Proverbs 22:9—The generous will themselves be blessed, for they share their food with the poor.

Closing Prayer

Pray with me:

"Father, by the power and authority You have, rebuke and dismantle the stronghold of mammon from my life. I ask that the stronghold of mammon not bear fruit in me ever again. God, with Your angelic armies, strip the power from this stronghold and free me from its grip. Lord of Hosts, I invite you to remove and uproot any way this stronghold has tormented my life as well as my family. Father God, carry this stronghold of mammon out now. Mammon, you will go to the place Jesus sends you and never return, in the name of Jesus Christ of Nazareth. Father, I give you permission to rewire my brain and change my thinking about the stronghold of mammon. Your Word says I have the mind of Christ (2 Corinthians 2:16); therefore, I shall have it.. I apply the blood of Jesus over my mind, and I have the mind of Christ. I have His thoughts. From this day forward, I am walking out my life with compassionate generosity. In Jesus' name I pray. Amen."

STRONGHOLD FIVE:
PREJUDICE

*"I look to a day when people will not be judged by the color of
their skin, but by the content of their character."*[10]
—*Martin Luther King Jr.*

MY STORY

As I have shared elsewhere, my grandmother's home in India was a place of honor and love. The way she managed her servants was with much kindness, respect, and dignity. However, that type of treatment was an exception to the culture in India. I did not realize the contrast until I went to visit one of my other wealthy relatives in another city.

I remember at the front of this relative's house was a large entrance with a locked gate. In front of that gate sat an impoverished lady in rags waiting for some money to be given to her. My heart was so moved with compassion. I wanted to give her everything I had. I remembered, however, being warned by my family members that I absolutely could not touch her as she was considered unclean.

Therefore, I would have to throw money at her, which didn't seem like the right thing to do. This uncompassionate, untouchable attitude is how many treat others in the lower castes. The caste that people are born into is the class they will be in the rest of their lives. They are expected to stay within the same social status until the day they die. People are not supposed to make progress in this life outside of their class. This unfair segregation and discrimination creates so much unnecessary pain and division between the poor and wealthy in the country. This societal system and the resulting type of treatment and prejudice is so normal in India that we all eventually become desensitized to it.

I also remember the shock I felt the first time I personally experienced prejudice when I came to the U.S. Some of my first-grade classmates teased me, calling me "brownie." Although America does not have a caste system like India, I felt such an oppression in that classroom that day. I think we all have a form of this stronghold flowing through our veins because of our fallen human nature. For children in first grade to do this to me shows that this prejudice or lack of appreciation of diversity is part of the sinful human nature. This behavior is not taught intentionally in these first graders' homes. I remember going home crying many days after school in first and second grade because I couldn't understand why my classmates didn't like me or celebrate me. They made me feel left out and rejected. I can remember feeling that something was wrong with the color of my skin at such a young age. I think it was important for me to feel the depth of the pain and the sting of discrimination so that I could better understand how my own prejudices hurt others. I got a taste of the very thing that was trying to grow in my own mind.

Years later, what I found most surprising about the stronghold of prejudice is that it can be established without us knowing it. Even various definitions of the word talk about the possible unknown characteristic of prejudice. According to the Cambridge Dictionary, *prejudice* is defined as an unfair or unreasonable opinion or feeling especially when formed without enough thought or knowledge.[11]

The Latin origin of the word prejudice literally means to prejudge. It means to make judgments in advance before actually knowing or understanding something or someone.[12]

Therefore, when we operate in the prejudice stronghold, we could either have a preconceived or perhaps an ill-informed perspective of another person or people group. Sometimes we have a combination of both. Either way, I believe that we are quick to criticize or prejudge people or things that we fear or don't understand. Prejudice may even be an unconscious form of self-protection.

When something is normalized in our culture, we tend to tolerate it and normalize it in our own lives. My judgments, however, built a prison in my mind that held me captive by the fear of a race that I did not know well. In America, the news media has greatly contributed to the creation of an unhealthy mindset toward African American culture. Growing up with news bombardment, I had written off this people group as mostly dangerous because that is what is constantly portrayed on the news. I began to believe that black males were especially dangerous and were not be trusted. With these messages, I grew up extremely fearful and did my best to avoid people from the "wrong side of the tracks."

We must be aware of the fact that the media is being used to divide us, perhaps now more than ever before. This stereotype of male African Americans being dangerous is extreme and untrue.

These messages combined with the societal caste system of my homeland led me to harbor a hidden prejudice. In my mind, I was condemning others in an unspoken manner without cause. Unknowingly, I felt this way toward African Americans, and I'm embarrassed to say that I deliberately didn't have any African American friends. It was not until I married Scott and heard his vision for the poor and compassion for the African American people that I first realized I had prejudice inside of me. I would have never imagined it, but my prejudice was undetected and unchallenged.

I also grew up with a culturally accepted form of socio-economic prejudice that should have kept me far away from places like the inner-city neighborhoods of Nashville. As I mentioned, prejudging people was a central tradition of my culture, and therefore it was a normal process in my brain, since that mentality labels, ranks, and segregates according to social class.

From this prejudicial hierarchy where everything is compared and sized up according to position and prominence in society, I was totally unprepared for my husband's vision that was inspired by reading the words of Jesus serving "the least of these." At first, as I mentioned in another chapter, my husband and his close friends had gotten involved in serving the poor with the homeless downtown Nashville, Tennessee. Seeing them serve was a stretch for me. But then, God showed that He was blessing their efforts. Not long after they started serving, they found a vacant building on the "wrong side town." This building could be renovated to become a home base to birth a nonprofit ministry. Their vision was to help alleviate the suffering and to provide the physical, emotional, and spiritual needs to people in the impoverished, underserved area of Nashville. When they started, this ministry was named Provision International. Today it is known as Harvest Sound International.

The ministry building was located in the area known as Hell's Half Acre that I've told you about previously. There was grocery store there where drug dealers hung out and the police raided. As I also mentioned earlier, the drug dealers placed bets on dog fights to make money. The building was near a government housing project also considered dangerous, known as Jo Johnston, which I also have discussed elsewhere in this book.

As you can imagine, I was struck with so much apprehension and anxiety when I thought about the idea of going into the government projects. When we were newlyweds, Scott asked if I would partner alongside him serving the poor and broken in this inner-city community. I was so scared and hesitant, but I loved and honored his noble heart, so I fearfully agreed to go with him. As I shared earlier in this book, I thought that either Scott or myself or both of us were going to die. The tremendous amount of fear that welled up in me literally paralyzed me, and I could not see straight. I tried to pray my fear away, but it would not leave. I had predetermined that there was nothing safe or good about these people who lived in these projects. I didn't understand them or their lifestyle. Fear mixed with prejudice had moved in and occupied the unknown.

FINDING MY FREEDOM

I began to catch a glimpse of what true freedom looked like by the way Scott lived his life. Scott had an unusual love for all races. This love, I believe, came from his parents raising him in a culture of kindness and celebration for all people. While Scott was growing up, his father, David MacLeod, was the president of Compassion International for Canada. Compassion serves impoverished children from all nationalities. His parents also hosted friends from diverse ethnic backgrounds from around the world in their home, showing hospitality. With his background, Scott didn't fear the "dangerous" Jo Johnston neighborhood in Nashville. His heart was so moved with compassion when he saw a people group secluded from the rest of the world without help or hope. I observed his positive perspective followed by his compassionate actions. He could see something that I couldn't see. Something was blinding me. *Would I be able to get free from this ancient stronghold of prejudice?*

I was faced with my husband's calling to minister to the inner-city, which confronted my fears of working with the African American race. Yes, our unbelievable God put this fearful Asian Indian in the middle of the hard-core, American inner-city community in Nashville, Tennessee. God must have looked at me and laughed seeing this playing out. He knew what was deeply hidden under my sweet personality. I found myself so ill-equipped and not trained to face what I would see. I knew that it was the hand of God that gave me the grace, vision, and stamina when, many times, I felt like giving up and running away. He knew that I needed to confront this prejudice stronghold in my life head on. I had to get free from my fear of the African American race and culture, but freedom came with a question: *Did I really trust God with my life, and could I surrender my life to Him no matter what happens in this inner city as I follow my husband?*

I was about to discover the answer to this question. As I fully surrendered my life to God, my fear of a people and culture that were totally unlike me began to lift. Praise God! I was becoming free!

Despite my fear diminishing, I still felt overwhelmed interacting with a community of people who had been corralled and segregated in government housing. They faced a mountain of issues: poverty, fatherlessness, worthlessness, teen pregnancy, gang initiation, drug sales, prostitution, and violence. I could feel an internal war inside of me. I did not realize the extent of my own insulation away from this culture. I had not been exposed to this part of society, and I found my personality so divergent from it.

When I held the precious babies in this community, however, deep wells of compassion within me began to overturn the years of prejudice that were built inside me stemming from my own culture and experience. I made a choice to love instead of judge.

I was finally able to get a clear understanding of my role in the vision my husband carried. As the Lord clarified what He had for me, I was reminded of a verse, which says, "Speak up for those who cannot speak up for themselves" (Proverbs 31:8). I then asked myself whom I need to speak up for, and I knew the answer. *I was to speak up for the babies and children trapped in hundreds of years of painful, dysfunctional, generational cycles.* These children did not choose the families they were born into. They did not choose generational dysfunction. They were born into poverty, sexual and verbal abuse, violence, prostitution, and drug addictions. All around them was an extraordinary amount of brokenness.

As we started to pray more about how to help this community, God gave us a strategy. He led us to infuse the single mothers with hope by helping them raise their children with unconditional love, by providing for their physical needs, and by renewing their minds with what God says about them. To break the hundreds of years of the effects of slavery and the physical, emotional, and spiritual bondage, we had to give them a fresh start and disciple them to change the course of their lives. These acts of love incrementally helped transform their lives and break the cycles of abandonment, addictions, and hopelessness.

Our strategy involved treating the children as our own and, in a sense, raising them from the youngest age possible. We lavished them with Christ's unfailing love and taught them biblical values such as honoring their parents and practicing forgiveness. We also taught them how much they are loved by God. We showed them how to speak truth over themselves using scriptures. The children would also memorize and pray these verses directly from the Word. With the collaboration of our staff, we developed a program called "Kids Club," which took place every Saturday morning from 9 a.m. to noon. Each child was picked up from his or her home and brought into an environment filled with love and hope. On average, we had about 150 to 200 children, ages three to 18, in Kids Club. They would run through our building called The Fortress of Hope. We trained our team captains and volunteers to disciple their group of kids each week by loving them, disciplining them when necessary, and instilling character based on biblical principles. Each team captain had an average of 12 kids he or she was directly in charge of to shepherd. This grouping allowed children to be known, loved, seen, esteemed, and encouraged each week.

The children left Kids Club with a homemade packed lunch and hearts overflowing with hope. We then encouraged each of them to go to their homes to invite their mothers, grandmothers, aunts, and uncles to a church service and a big family barbecue, both of which we held every Saturday.

Before and during each week's church service, I would gather a handful of people in our church family, and we would pray for several hours. I remember praying and declaring weekly that one day God will bring a full restoration to our devastated Jo Johnston community. I remember praying Isaiah 58:12, "Father God, would You help us rebuild the ancient ruins of John Henry Hale, and would You help us raise up the age-old foundations? And would You help us restore these streets and dwellings?"

Our actions loving this "dangerous" community was inspired by Romans 12:21, which implores us not to be overcome with evil but to overcome evil with good. This scripture spoke to us about the importance of offering hope in place of brokenness, and God responded to our faith actions. We opened our storehouses weekly and gave out food boxes, clothing, and furniture. In addition, we sent our staff out to do weekly visitations to check on families in our community. Every Thursday evening, we prepared a love feast for our children and families in Jo Johnston, and we called it the Meal of Hope. Meal of Hope not only nourishes each guest's body with food, but it also nourished each guest's soul, and spirit with God's great love and His Living Hope. These evenings are comprised of eating good food together, listening to good music, sharing stories, praying, and sharing the Good News of His living, abundant hope, which the guests are invited to receive as they put their trust in Jesus. The meal and the message shared lets them know that God loves them, that God has great plans for them, and that He has not forgotten them in their struggles. When people are hopeless, the Gospel of Jesus is the greatest source of hope.

The key to overcoming poverty is not just giving people a meal or providing material things. We have to give them hope. It's only hope that will allow them to endure through their difficulties and suffering. In addition to the Thursday meal, we have an evangelism and worship night every Friday night, which we call Fireplace.

We learned that we can have a greater level of empathy and compassion by walking in others' shoes and entering into their world. Being let into this community's world is a privilege Scott and I had. We read scriptures and obeyed even when we did not understand. One of the passages that was particularly meaningful was

> The Spirit of the sovereign LORD is on me, because the LORD has anointed me to proclaim good news to the poor. He has sent me to bind up the brokenhearted, to proclaim freedom for the captives and release from darkness for the prisoners…(Isaiah 61:1).

The beauty was that, as I chose to obey God's standard, I was able to see the gold and the treasures in these little ones as well as in their families. I would have missed the beauty in these precious kids had God not been working to remove my hurtful, prejudicial lens.

Transformation Takes Time

I knew the work that God called Scott and I to do was to help rebuild, restore, and transform this community so that the generations ahead would have a new beginning and strong foundation. I did not think that this restoration would happen in our lifetime. God showed us that we were like farmers planting much good seed into these orphans, widows, single mothers, and their loved ones. We would then nourish this seed in an environment filled with life, love, hope, and good deeds. God also showed us that one day, a massive harvest of righteousness with these lives would come, and the entire the region would transform.

I have to admit that it was a lonely season, and at times, I have felt like an emergency responder with no equipment or support to help. Also, many people we had known living in the suburbs judged us for wanting to help the inner-city community. They didn't understand why we would leave our high-paying jobs to go serve in the inner city. Instead of supporting us as we had hoped, they seemed indifferent, apathetic, or perplexed. These friends did not lend a helping hand to lift the load that we carried day after day. They often did not see the value in helping people who were dangerous, or who, according to them, just needed to get a job. The mindset was that helping poor African Americans is a waste of time. I didn't blame these friends; they were only living out what they had been conditioned to think. Sadly, many churches in our city hadn't had a vison for missionary work in inner city either: missions were focused overseas. We needed local help to break the generational dysfunctions and pain of these underserved families. We needed a compassionate army ready to rescue to help those desperate and dying.

The thousands of little ones in the inner cities of our country are like treasures or diamonds in our midst; they are precious and need care that fits their value as Christ's sons and daughters. They need physical, emotional, and spiritual support to be strengthened, flourish, and thrive in society. Even though the laws of the land changed to bring freedom for the African Americans from slavery, they have had to find freedom without the necessary tools to heal their hearts and minds from an enslaved mindset. Bringing this freedom takes people who have broken through the prejudice mindset believing in them and setting value on who they are. Only people who have found this freedom can help to heal the hearts and minds of these impoverished communities. Neither time nor new laws can totally heal the effects of discrimination. Members of these inner-city or forgotten communities need tools to break the trauma, pain, shame, devastation, and stigmas of racism, as well as kind-hearted people to come alongside and support them along the way.

Week after week, year after year, broken lives were made whole and transformed. It took several years for this community to trust us that we were there genuinely there *for* them—and to believe that we were not there to use them because the Jo Johnston community hadn't received help for generations. They were accustomed to having people come for a day to see them as a project that would satisfy their civic duty to serve the poor. These people who were serving for a day, however, didn't take the time to understand what the inner-city community members were going through as individuals.

Only after we had established trust with the families did they begin to open their hearts to receive our help and guidance. When they began to believe we were on their side cheering them on consistently, and they saw that we were dedicated to helping their families prosper, they let their guards down. Fears began to melt, and these precious children and their families were able to receive healing and break cycles of mistrust, addictions, and abuse. In other words, we were able to infuse hope into these single mothers and children. They began to have renewed identities, and instead of living with an abandoned mindset, they began to see themselves as God sees them—as valuable, loved, and important.

Life comes full circle when we choose to bless people, races, and cultures that are different from ours. This reciprocation happened in my life, as our family received blessings far beyond what words can describe. The following stories demonstrate the love we received, and they make me tear up thinking about them.

Dorothy's Influence

One of our dearest single mothers in Jo Johnston, whom I met in 1996, was a lady named Dorothy. She had the kindest heart and the most beautiful smile. She had three children. I was especially close with one of them named Kelly. We served Dorothy and helped invest in her children with weekly visitations, prayer, food, and discipleship. Kelly was part of Harvest Sound International's dance school. As the children got older, they moved away, and I had not seen them in years.

In April 2020, I was in desperate need of a trusted, safe health care worker to take care of my mother in the night hours from 11p.m. to 6 a.m. These were the hours that my mother was awake because she had severe dementia. She had lost her memory, and in this impaired mental state, she thought all her family members were her enemies, which can be a normal part of the disease.

During this extraordinarily painful time, my siblings and I struggled to handle the care of my mother in the early morning hours by ourselves. To help, we hired a lovely lady named Erica, who was recommended by one of our family friends. Amazingly though, Erica is the niece of Dorothy. Erica was mentored and strengthened in the faith by Dorothy, whom we had invested in years before she had passed away. Erica came and took the night shift, and she had the patience, compassion, and understanding to care for my mother in the midst of her dementia meltdowns.

Those were some dark times; my siblings and father were mentally and physically exhausted from taking care of my mother day and night. With Erica's consistent patience, love, and care for my mother, we were all able to work together and help my mother. My mother is now fully healed and thriving. This story is a full circle of love and redemption from helping a single mother and children, who God then used to help heal my own family.

Rhonda's Story

As I got untangled from this prejudice mindset, I learned to connect with people who were not like me. Diversity in our relationships is important so that we can see people who are different from us without eyes of judgment, but instead, with understanding. I know God gave me a gift of discernment, but I have to be careful to discern and not judge, critiquing people and their motives without knowing their heart or intentions. I may discern that something is not right or even evil, but that does not mean that person is evil. This situation happened to me one time when I was working and planning ways to love our Jo Johnston Community. An annual event we did was called Luncheon of Love, which was a special time for us to celebrate and value single mothers. We prepared a delicious feast set on beautiful China with lovely silverware. We also collected gifts for each of the women, such as designer clothes, shoes, which these ladies would not normally be able to afford. In addition, we did hair and makeup for all the ladies before lunch began.

A young woman, Rhonda, approached me after I spoke at the luncheon. She was clearly distressed and desperate for advice. She was a tall, slender woman in her early 30s with big brown eyes and the most radiant smile. She said that she already had five children, and the sixth child was on the way. She said she could not keep her baby, because she was already struggling to take care of the other five. She was living with her boyfriend at the time, and she proceeded to tell me that she was planning to abort the baby. I was at first very disturbed that she would think about this option, and I could have judged her for being insensitive and cruel in making the decision to kill her baby. But instead of prejudging, I put myself in her shoes to understand that she was in a lot of emotional pain, trying to cope the best way she knew how.

With a heart of love—not judgment—I prayed with her and asked God to show her what she should do. I encouraged her to keep the baby and to pray. I also told her that if she chose to keep the baby, I would help her through the pregnancy and support her every way I could. At that luncheon, I also shared my faith in Jesus and invited her to let Him into her life. She chose that day to let Jesus help her walk through this lonely, confusing, painful time. I was quite stunned that she felt that she could trust me enough to share her dilemma and heart with me.

Two weeks later, Rhonda came to me and said she had made up her mind. She had decided to keep the baby instead of aborting! My whole body was flooded with so much joy! I felt like crying, but I held back my tears. I told her that I was so proud of her for making this decision, and I started preparing to raise funds to bring this baby into the world.

I reached out to my friends who lived in the suburbs, telling them Rhonda's story. Many women contributed generous financial gifts and presents, which we lavished on Rhonda at a surprise baby shower. She received baby blankets, strollers, car seats, diapers, and more. I was overwhelmed by the generosity of many women who contributed to help Rhonda. She was so surprised and abundantly blessed.

With God's help, I was able to help Rhonda rewrite her generational past and pave a new path for her future. With our Kids Club mentoring program, we also taught her children honor, truth, kindness, and purity, and we helped to reaffirm their value. We helped them break unhealthy generational patterns and mindsets. I had the privilege of walking with Rhonda and discipling her and her children for many years.

With the love of Jesus and through His truth, we broke her feelings of guilt, shame, failure, and unworthiness. Over time, I watched her life, and the lives of her children transform. They became joy-filled and strong in their identities. After intentionally investing in Rhonda's life for three years, I could say that Rhonda knew she was a beautiful, smart, capable woman who did not live with a poverty mentality. She worked hard and got a job she enjoyed. She was promoted into a management position. I remember running into Rhonda many years later after she had moved away. She expressed her profound gratitude for the ways I invested in her whole family.

How Helping These Women and Children Changed Me

If I had stayed in my safe prejudiced bubble where I only associated with people like me from my own social class, I would not have been able to be part of Rhonda's life transformation or the joy that her changed life brought. I do not think her life transformation would have happened if I had not let go of criticism and judgment so that I could understand what Rhonda was going through to help bridge the gap through love and trust. This love came not through me, but from Jesus Christ, who willingly bled and died for me and for the healing and restoration of all of humanity. Nor would I have been able to bless Rhonda through people in the suburbs who previously didn't want to help. My suburb and community were influenced by how I had changed and the joy I had found from my inner-city community. I believe as we change and break free from strongholds that hold us captive, including prejudice, we will be able to influence others to also break free because the way we live our lives becomes examples.

Freedom and a New Identity for Our Community

As stated before, in 2006, on the 50th year of when the Jo Johnston community was built, our dream for the inner city to be transformed came to pass. The Jo Johnston housing project received a $27 million grant called the HOPE Grant, which was one way God was showing us we are on track with His heart for His people. I never imagined that our community would get this Hope grant. It was especially miraculous to receive this grant on the 50th "Jubilee" year of the community. God is precise with timing and His timing is perfect.

It was so appropriate that the grant was named "HOPE!" Hope allows people to see beyond their devastating circumstances. It provokes them not to give up or settle in their situation. Ultimately, we connected them to the One who can give them this lifelong hope and a future. As a Christian community, we believe Jesus is the LIVING hope, and if we follow His ways, we will always have hope.

After the redevelopment of this community made possible by God though years of prayers and service—and the grant—the area, previously known by some as Hell's Half Acre, was renamed and transformed into Rainbow Row by new business owners who came to establish themselves in the community. New rainbow-colored houses were built, and businesses, attracted by the historic buildings in the area and the lower crime rates, began to open and improve the area. What a transformation and a picture of God's promise, since God uses the rainbow to represent new life after the flood! (In case you are unfamiliar with the biblical account of the rainbow, I invite you to read Genesis 9.)

This community was destined to stay enslaved, but as I, along with many others, stepped out in faith and broke out of our comfort zones and prejudices, I saw the Jo Johnston community through God's eyes. **God then made our community into a glorious display of His splendor, demonstrating His transformation and promises fulfilled—from darkness to light, from violence to peace, from hopeless to hope-filled, from surviving to thriving, and from enslaved to set free!**

I said it before, but it is worth repeating: Our vision and dream came true. Because we were determined not to look out for our own interests, but instead, to fight for an oppressed, underserved, and neglected people group, we watched the manifestation of promises fulfilled. I believe this transformation is just the beginning. I know that God is wanting to do some additional marvelous works to continue to build upon this Jubilee. As I have said elsewhere in this book, I believe what is coming next is a Renaissance, or a rebirth of arts, intellect, and education in our inner-city community as well as impoverished communities all over the US and across the world.

As I look back on what has happened in our community, I see how the foundation of Christ's love was reflected in everything that happened. The prejudice stronghold can perpetuate division between rich and poor, but Jesus says that the first will be last and the last will be first (Matthew 20:16). He valued and honored the most broken and vulnerable, and He calls us to imitate what he modeled for us. He does not see us with eyes that condemn because of race, color, gender, culture, appearance, or even the bad things we have done. We are new creations when we receive His precious Spirit. His fresh Living Water is poured into our lives to wash the stench of the world and its prejudice off us.

I learned that brokenness is a common denominator among all races. I've learned that LOVE binds us together. The power of blessing and taking action steps to break out of prejudice will bring with it a profound reciprocation. I believe breaking free from this stronghold will bring restoration as well as abundance not only for the people you bless but also for your own life. I want to equip people to break free together from prejudice and live a life of love. But first, I need to share more about how this sometimes-hidden stronghold takes root.

EXPOSING THE STRONGHOLD

This section will help you see the potential trap of the prejudice stronghold, both for yourself and for society at large.

When we have prejudice, we have already decided on how we will view or treat a person. In essence, we have made a judgment about that person without knowing his or her individual character, perhaps based on a racial or ethnic stereotype. Jesus says in Matthew, "For the same way you judge others, you will be judged, and with the measure you use, it will be measured to you" (Matthew 7:2). Said another way, this scripture is stating that as we make a premature assessment about someone, we have not only placed a judgement on his or her life, but we also have placed a judgement on our own lives. Because of the spiritual law of sowing and reaping, these judgements can actually harm us. If we think less of others, we may be opening a door, unknowingly, to have others judge us.

Before we go much further, we would be wise to consider if this stronghold may be affecting each of us. Therefore, I encourage you to ask yourself the following questions:

- Do I tend to get more easily frustrated by people who have a different skin color than I do?
- Do I have any racial stereotypes pop up in my mind when I see a person who has a different skin color than I do?
- Am I open to forming close friendships with those who look and act differently than me?

If you answered yes to these questions, you may be in bondage to this stronghold. You will have a chance to assess your life more fully and to use the tools to secure your freedom at the end of this chapter. First, however, I want you to see how widespread and devastating the effects of this stronghold are. I've found this information helps people realize that they are not alone—and you aren't either! If we all do our part to dismantle this stronghold, the entire world could change!

In this section, we will look at how prejudice has infiltrated India, the U.S., and the world. First, though, I have to say that, regardless of culture, no one has the right to judge another person by their color or their race. According to Proverbs 22:2, we are created by a master designer who loves each of us equally. We as humans did not create the human race, so what gives us the right to judge, criticize, discriminate, segregate, alienate, or shame people who are different from us or weaker than us?

Fostering this pre-judgment of others based on their circumstances, economic status, intellect, or skin color is an evil plot orchestrated by the enemy, Satan. The adversary is at work to divide the human race and conquer it through this sometimes subtle stronghold, which includes unconscious biases, inequality, and pre-judgements. These judgments that we make about other humans based on color, race, religion, disability, social status, age, and gender need to be discerned so we can come out of our self-induced curses as well as come out from under the control of an evil adversary who will pit us against each other and divide us. Let's now look at some specific examples of this stronghold at work.

In India

Throughout India, there historically has been and there still is a tremendous amount of prejudice based on appearance, level of intelligence, job, caste, wealth, and education level. If that weren't enough, Asian Indians also judge each other by the complexion of a person's skin. Light-skinned Indians get more favor than dark-skinned Indians, and when you are picking marriage partners for your children, it's preferable in many Asian Indian's minds that these future spouses be light-skinned.

Even if you are a practicing Christian in India you are still labeled (and label others) by social (rich, middle-class, or poor), instead of being placed in a specific caste like you would be if you were Hindu. However, the idea of judging by wealth is the same regardless of religion. As I've said elsewhere, in the 3,000-year-old Hindu caste system, your caste determines your occupation. Castes are ranked from highest to lowest. Brahmins, the highest caste, are the priests and scholars of society, and Shudras, the lowest caste, are the laborers. Below the Shudras are the Dalits, formerly known as the "untouchables," who are often outcast by India's society. They are considered so unworthy that they don't fall within the caste system. Historically this group of people was assigned the dirtiest jobs, such as cleaning sewers, tanning leather, or removing dead animals from the streets. Despite caste discrimination being outlawed in India's newest constitution written in 1950, an unfair stigma remains on the Dalits.[13] No matter what level of education the Dalits receive or what occupation they secure, the Dalits are still, in modern day, held captive by cultural judgements.

The Hindu religion prohibits them from breaking out of the caste because the belief is that they deserve such treatment because of sins they committed during their previous lives. This belief that the lowest castes deserve their fate ensures that often they are treated with an extraordinary amount of prejudice. As a result, little social interaction occurs between the highest and middle castes with the lowest caste. In addition, there is minimal effort to help this group out of their difficult situation because this prejudice stronghold being so prevalent.

The prejudiced mindset against those in other classes permeates so much of culture that breaking through this stronghold is difficult because doing so would completely dismantle societal norms and biases. Even in an Indian arranged marriage, the selection of a child's future spouse is determined by the caste that that child is born into. People are not allowed to marry outside of his or her caste or class. Sadly, I don't think this type of prejudice, which includes exclusion and discrimination, is intentional for Asian Indians. Many of us have been raised to think this way. Exclusion is so normal and accepted in the Indian culture that I personally thought it was quite normal until I came to the realization that it was wrong.

In the U.S.

Beyond myself and my story, which crosses over two nations, the stronghold of prejudice has gripped people across time and ethnic groups. History tells the stories of the destruction and pain of prejudice which can leave lasting devastation for generations to come. That is what happened to two people groups in the U.S.— the Native Americans being displaced from their land in America and the African Americans in slavery.

Today's bait of prejudice wears the disguise of stereotypes, mistrust, and blame in our society. Negative incidents among cultures or races are often magnified by the media.

New traumas reopen the previously healed wounds of historical discrimination. When these old wounds are reopened without the tools to heal people's hearts, these wounds may trigger additional anger and hate. This pattern only perpetuates a never-ending circle of prejudice. In 2020, the media exploited the circumstances of George Floyd's death, although it was obviously senseless and tragic. It was used to turn African Americans against white Americans. In fact, this incident reinjured a national wound that had been healing for decades. I believe we need to learn from history, so that we do not repeat the same mistakes. We need to let go of mistrust, stereotyping, and instead choose to use the God given tools of love and forgiveness to reconcile with those that have hurt or mistreated us.

Depending on the government to help with issues of poverty and injustice, as history has shown us, does not end well. Welfare, which in America is a range of government programs to provide financial aid and other services for those who cannot support themselves, perpetuates an inferiority mindset and sets those who have it up to stay trapped in their social class. The welfare system is not fair, and too often, it creates an unhealthy dependence on government programs, making it difficult for members of the low-income population to break out of poverty without shifting their mindsets.

However, I have personally witnessed that it is absolutely possible for these people to break free from this welfare system by being empowered to work hard using their God-given abilities.

All of Humanity

The entire human race was created by God, who created us to be equal. **Prejudice and all that comes with it including racism,**

biases, judgments, and segregation are human sin issues, not skin issues. It seems that many races have the innate ability to oppress others because of personal biases. Although we talked about Adolf Hitler in another chapter because he misused knowledge, he was clearly propagating prejudice as well when he espoused a discriminating mindset that led him to have millions of Jews exterminated. He knew how to use political propaganda, and he manipulated and controlled others using the tools of violence and terror. Without keen awareness of this stronghold and discernment that comes from our Creator who made us all equal, mankind will inevitably destroy ourselves with division. We have the capability to discriminate against others or to turn on others, which ultimately brings destruction. I believe, however, with Gods help we will not be overcome by this deceptive prejudice stronghold.

Although Hitler's prejudice seems obvious in hindsight, some forms of prejudice may not be as apparent or realized. In the Bible, favoritism, for example, is a sin against God. James 2:9 says, "…if you show favoritism, you sin and are convicted by the law as lawbreakers." Favoritism is a sin because it is inconsistent with the character of God. As people, we tend to show favoritism and put others in stratified categories similar to how castes stratify the Asian Indian population. In addition to race and class, we categorize people by their clothes, cars, religion, denomination, gender, and culture. Regardless of where our prejudice originated, we all have a choice to make to eradicate it from our lives.

ESCAPING THE STRONGHOLD

This section is your invitation to break free so you can live free.

These issues that we've discussed around prejudice are wrong and devilish. They must be uncovered, exposed, and brought into the light. The good news is that escaping this stronghold is possible! I have seen it first-hand! And God is extending His invitation for us to embrace this freedom to each of us! What's even more amazing is that as we choose freedom individually, our choices collectively may lead to freedom on a larger scale—first for our families, then our communities, then our countries, then our world!

First things, first, though. If we are to eradicate racial inequality on a national scale, we must start with introspection of our individual lives, the choices of our social circles, and how we conduct ourselves with people different from us. We must take personal responsibility for our lives, and that responsibility starts with making healthy choices on how we deal with the pain and injustice of inequality.

We need to uproot the prejudice mindset from our lives and celebrate the beauty of diversity instead of discriminating against people. We cannot waste time just talking about it; let's start helping those who are in need, even if they are different from us.

We must come together for the sake of the survival of the future generations and the preservation of our beautiful world.

Enough is enough. Prejudice has taken enough prisoners on all sides, through indoctrination, enslavement, or victimization.

Let's not allow healthy oneness to be diminished or stolen because of prejudice and unforgiveness being harbored in our hearts. Jesus gave us tools to heal intentional and unintentional pain. He can heal our pasts, but we MUST choose to love and forgive those who have hurt us so that we can receive love in our hearts and expel bitterness, fear, and hate. Perfect love casts out fear. We can win this class and color war with LOVE.

Let's break out of the captivity of critical views, venomous speech, and hostile behaviors. Let's break free together from prejudice and live a life of love. Let's love out loud with our actions.

Let's dream with God for people and areas that have been forgotten, marginalized, or neglected. God fulfilled my husband's and my audacious dream with a simple "yes" to follow him. He gave us steadfast perseverance and the ability to not give up when it was hard. He gave us the ability to see others who were not like us with eyes of compassion and steadfast love that perseveres through difficulties instead of being bound by this ugly prejudice stronghold.

I want to encourage you to dream some God-sized dreams! He wants to bring your big, audacious dreams to fruition—just like He did for us!

To take the first step in escaping this stronghold, read through the list in the next section and earnestly look for these identifiers of prejudice in your life. You too can break free and live free experiencing the joy, unity, and celebration of diverse cultures. Then He can use you to make an impact in many lives as He makes your "impossible dreams" come true!

ASSESSING YOURSELF

Prejudice Identifiers

For each stronghold, 20 identifiers are listed. As you read, put a check mark by the ones you feel apply to you. Each check mark will be considered one point. Add up the check marks, which will give you the total points for this stronghold. By the end of this book, you will be able to rank which stronghold needs the most attention first by the greatest number of points. (Most people have some of each; if this happens to you, don't be discouraged. God will enable you to break free of every stronghold—it just may take some time.)

1. I tend to spend time with people who look and act like me.
2. I tend to feel that my race is the best.
3. I tend to despise people who have a darker complexion or lighter complexion than me.
4. I tend to judge people quickly without getting to know them.
5. I tend to have difficulty building relationships with people unlike me.
6. I tend to have difficulty learning from someone who is another race or gender.
7. I tend to practice a religion that discriminates against people based on race, the gender that they are born as, socioeconomic class, or color of skin.
8. I tend to believe I am part of the superior race.
9. I tend to get anxious when I have to be with people who do not act like me.
10. When I travel to a new country, I tend to not learn the culture as I know the way my culture dresses and acts is the best.

11. I tend to despise a certain group of people.

12. I tend to categorize people instead of seeing people as individuals, such as judging people by where they live, what type of car they drive, or what type of clothes they wear.

13. I tend to not have hope or vision for an oppressed or distressed people group.

14. I tend to make jokes or make fun of people that are different from me.

15. I tend not to have much emotion when I meet new people.

16. I tend not to help people that are a different social class than me.

17. I tend not to date anyone other than my race.

18. I tend to think it's better for me or my family members to marry within the same socioeconomic class.

19. I tend to criticize people easily and think negatively.

20. I tend to have intolerance to people different from me.

Reflection Questions

Take a few moments to get quiet and think about the following reflection questions and write your answers in a journal.

1. Have you encountered the prejudice stronghold in your life? How did it negatively affect the people around you?

2. What symptoms of the prejudice stronghold have you noticed in your life?

3. Was there a part of my story that you related to in your own life?

4. On a scale of 0–10, how would you rate your level of acceptance you have for other races and nationalities? (Zero is no acceptance and 10 is the best you could possibly do).

5. What two action steps can you take to actualize healing with those affected by prejudice around you? (For example: establish intentional relationships, ask for and listen to their experiences, serve underserved communities such as a Native American reservation or an inner-city ministry in meaningful capacities).

STEPPING INTO YOUR FREEDOM

If you recognize this prejudice mindset in yourself, below are some clear steps to take so that you dismantle the chains that have tried to imprison you. The first thing is to repent, which means to turn completely in the opposite direction of it.

Repent

Pray with me:

"God I'm so sorry. I repent for every way I partnered with the prejudice mindset and allowed the stronghold of prejudice to rule my life, my decisions, and my beliefs. Your Word says to take every thought captive to the obedience of Christ. I am taking this stronghold of prejudice captive and no longer allowing it to confine or ensnare me."

Renounce

To renounce a stronghold is to break agreement with toxic beliefs that have formed a stronghold. When we renounce something, we make a declaration that we no longer affiliate with that system of beliefs.

Break agreements with the following statements that apply to you. I break agreement with the stronghold of prejudice because:

- I was quick to judge others.
- I have an intolerance for people that look act or believe differently than me.

- I was captivated by fear of people who look act or believe differently than me.
- I am quick to judge and criticize people when they behave or look or believe differently than me.
- I lack empathy for those that seem different than me.
- I don't need to help people that are oppressed or distressed.
- I walked in pride thinking I was superior to those different.
- I did not see people with the eyes of love or goodwill.

Declare with me:

"I renounce and break all agreements I have made with the stronghold of prejudice and my attachment to living with the prejudiced stronghold as a way of life.

Specifically, I renounce the judgments, intolerance, pride, and critical heart I have set for people who look, act, or believe differently than me. I also renounce the beliefs of prejudice found in the statements above that I have just broken agreement with. I am so sorry, God, for coming into agreement with a stronghold of prejudice and how I have lived my life based on the effects of this prejudice mindset. Please forgive me, Father God, for not seeing people with eyes of love and good will."

Release

Pray with me:

"Father God, I release this prejudice stronghold and place it at Your feet. Break me free from all the ways the stronghold of prejudice has affected my life and those around me. Eradicate any unhealthy judgments I have placed on people around me or people groups

different than me. Forgive me for being critical and intolerant of people different than me. Today I choose to see people with Your eyes. Eyes that see with compassion, empathy, and love. I choose to hear and understand different perspectives than mine. Today I choose to see that all people are valuable and have treasures inside them. Jesus, I plead Your blood over my life and the stronghold of prejudice. Remove me from the grip of this stronghold and release me from its effects. I receive the power of Your blood to wash and renew me today."

Restore

Pray with me:

"Father God, what do You want to give me in place of prejudice? How should I live out my life differently now that I no longer agree with the stronghold of prejudice?

Listen carefully and journal what God speaks to you. When you let go of something that was not healthy or good, God always replaces it with good things. So, thank God for this good gift and walk out your life with it.

Rewire

Say with me:

- "I am choosing this day to live my life breaking out of ungodly judgments of people. Instead, I am choosing to live with love and acceptance.
- I am living from this day forward loving people who are different from me, and I look forward to building bridges of healing and reconciliation.

- I am choosing to take responsibility for the way I have treated people, and I will not blame others or live in self-pity.

- I am living in the fulfillment of every promise God has for my life.

- I am overturning the demonic tactics that the enemy has put in my life through the stronghold of prejudice.

- I am unraveling the effects of prejudice in my life and family bloodline.

- I am choosing to love and speak up for those who are broken because of the effects of this prejudice stronghold.

- I am choosing to understand even when it is difficult."

Scriptures to Meditate on

- Matthew 7:1–2—"Do not judge, or you too will be judged. ²For in the same way you judge others, you will be judged, and with the measure you use, it will be measured to you."

- James 2:1–4—My brothers, show no partiality as you hold the faith in the Lord Jesus Christ, the Lord of glory. For if a man wearing a gold ring and fine clothing comes into your assembly and poor man in shabby clothing also comes in and if you pay attention to the one who wears the fine clothing and say, "Here's a good seat for you," while you say to the poor man, "You stand there," or "Sit on the floor at my feet," have you not discriminated among yourselves and become judges with evil thoughts?

- James 2:8–9—If you really keep the royal law found in Scripture, 'Love your neighbor as yourself,' you are doing right. But if you show favoritism you commit sin.

- 1 Peter 4:8—Above all, love each other deeply, because love covers over a multitude of sins.

- 1 Corinthians 13:13—And now these three remain: faith, hope and love. But the greatest of these is love

- Colossians 3:13—Bear with each other and forgive one another if any of you has a grievance against someone. Forgive as the Lord forgave you.

- 1 John 4:19–2—We love because he first loved us. Whoever claims to love God yet hates a brother or sister is a liar. For whoever does not love their brother and sister, whom they have seen, cannot love God, whom they have not seen. And he has given us this command: Anyone who loves God must also love their brother and sister whom they have seen, cannot love God, whom they have not seen.

Closing Prayer

"Father, by the power and authority You have, would You rebuke and dismantle the stronghold of PREJUDICE from my life. I ask that this stronghold of prejudice would not bear fruit ever again in me. God, with Your angelic armies, strip the power from this stronghold of prejudice and free me from its grip. Lord of Hosts, I invite You to remove and uproot any way the stronghold of prejudice has tormented my life as well as the lives of my family. Father God, carry this stronghold of prejudice out now. This stronghold will go to the place Jesus sends it, and never return, in the name of Jesus Christ of Nazareth. Father, I give you permission to rewire my brain and to change my thinking about thoughts that lead to this prejudice stronghold. You Word says I have the mind of Christ (1 Corinthians 2:16); therefore, I shall have it. I apply the blood of Jesus over my

mind, and I have the mind of Christ; I have his thoughts. In Jesus'
name I pray. Amen."

LIVING FREE

Living free is my hope and dream for each of you. For those of you who have prayed the prayers found in these chapters, congratulations. You have taken the first step to break free so that you can live free. You will begin, if you haven't already, experiencing your newfound freedom!

What can you expect this freedom to look like as you continue to walk it out?

- Instead of being bound by the stronghold of dead religion, you will continue to live free by having a vibrant, active, and eternal relationship with the Living God.

- Instead of being stuck under the stronghold of performance, you will continue live free embodying a spirit of excellence and fulfilling your divine design.

- Instead of being strangled by a stronghold of humanistic knowledge, you will continue to live free receiving wisdom and revelation directly from God, walking in His most excellent ways, and fulfilling His dreams for your life.

- Instead of being bound by the stronghold of mammon, you will continue to live free trusting in God's provision for generosity and multiplication.
- Instead of being bound by the stronghold of prejudice, you will continue to live free, unbiased with love and acceptance for every individual.

What if each of us used this magnificent freedom to find just one person that we could selflessly serve today? Think how that life would be impacted by our love, kindness, and attention.

What if each of us invested in the greatest treasures we have on Earth—the people and relationships that God has placed in our lives to steward?

What if each of us used more of our material resources sacrificially to feed the poor and lift up the afflicted instead of only taking care of ourselves and our families?

What if more of us freely received what Jesus went to the cross and died for, such as His love, forgiveness, and healing, so that we no longer walk in shame, apathy, depression, anxiety, or fear?

What if the two billion people who have identified themselves as Christians had a vibrant relationship with Jesus and truly knew the love of their Father God and then boldly lived out their faith?

If each of us said "yes" to these "what if" scenarios, our world would look far different. The widows and orphans would be cared for, and each of us would experience peace and joy as we live out the precious time we have been given here on this earth. Our cities, our nation, and our world would be flooded with an abundance of love and joy.

Therefore, it's time we trusted God to protect us and care for us as we go to love the most vulnerable people in our neighborhoods and surrounding cities.

And it's time we treated everyone whom we cross paths with genuine love and kindness knowing that each individual has infinite value.

~

I can already envision you having ongoing breakthrough from each of these strongholds that once held you captive. I can see you loosed to infiltrate our society and discover the abundant life you were meant to live. I can see you free to love…free to laugh…free to live. Together, for the rest of our lives, let's break free and live free.

SEALING PRAYER

Lord God, thank You for waking us out of our slumber, away from the ensnarement of these strongholds! Help us continue to understand that we no longer have to live—or go back to the captivity of—these strongholds. Let us continue to apply the authority that You have invested in us. Thank You that You will sustain and love us with Your everlasting love, which will never fail us. Let us always embrace Your courage, boldness, and joy as we run freely into the mission for which you have called us. Let freedom reign!

Based on Isaiah 60:1–3, pray and declare these words over yourself, your family, and your nation:

"Arise, shine (insert your name, your family members' names, or your nation's name here), Your light has come and the glory of the Lord rises upon (insert your name, your family members' names, or your nation's name here). The Lord rises upon (insert your name, your family members' names, or your nation's name here) and His

glory appears over (insert your name, your family members' names, or your nation's name here). Nations will come to Your light and kings to the brightness of Your dawn. In Jesus' name I pray. Amen."

APPENDIX
KNOWING CHRIST

If you have not accepted Jesus Christ and received salvation through Him, today is the day. All that is needed is to believe in your heart and speak with your mouth that He is Lord. You can pray this now:

> *"Jesus, I recognize You as Lord of my life. I repent for my past sins and unbelief. I surrender my life to You now. Receive me into Your Kingdom and fill me with Your Holy Spirit."*

Let us move forward together now in a new understanding of our relationship with God and in the freedom and power available to us in Him.

ACKNOWLEDGMENTS

I want to specifically thank the people that had a role in helping me get this book written and brought to completion.

I have been blessed abundantly to have a family that loves and supports me through all the joys and trials of life. I want to especially thank my husband, Scott, my daughter, Emily, and my son, Daniel. You all are my greatest cheerleaders. You more than anyone else know the time it took through these years to get this book done and the need to be flexible with all our schedules. Thank you for your loving support and daily sacrifices.

I am ever so grateful for my loving father and mother, Dr. Thomas and Mary John, who have embodied strength and perseverance in order to pave a path for myself, as well as all their children, so we could flourish. I am forever thankful for their steadfast faith in Christ and the many sacrifices they have made on my behalf to fulfill the call on my life. I love you with all my heart.

I also want to thank my husband's mother and father, Dave and Lyla MacLeod, who have set a standard and example of a godly kingdom family with kingdom principles.

This book was sparked in my heart and then ignited when my friend Jean Tannehill said, "Sarah you have a book in you, and you need to write your story." Thank you Jean for your love, support, and vision for this book.

I want to thank Amy Ford, one of my first editors, who sat patiently with me for almost a year as I wrote chapter after chapter. I could not have written this book without your help, wisdom and insight.

I also want to thank my final editor, Loral Pepoon, who patiently challenged and fine-tuned my book. I acknowledge your expertise, professionalism, and guidance.

I want to thank my photographer Emily Anne Photo Art, who has an impeccable eye to create beauty.

I want to thank my dear friends Suzanne, Cindy, and Rebecca, who steadfastly cheer me on consistently. I love you!

I want to thank all our Harvest Sound staff who encouraged me and made many sacrifices so I can take time to write.
I also want to thank one of my favorite advocates, Courtney Cordes, who is now cheering me on from Heaven. I love you with all my heart! I have watched her break free from each one of these strongholds.

I also want to thank our Harvest Sound church family, elders, and board who carry and embody a culture of breaking free and living free from the strongholds written in this book. What a privilege to be able to run with perseverance the race that is marked out before us to see the greatest global harvest.

ABOUT ME

I'm so glad you have read this book.

I hope you can tell that I feel an urgency for people to understand and live from their God-given identity and negate the lies the world, media, and culture are sending out every day.

Jesus told us in John 15 that He is the vine, and we are the branches. Therefore, He is the source of our healing, strength, and purpose in life.

As you have also likely surmised as you have read this book, I am passionate about helping people identify the roots of their pain, trauma, and strongholds, so that they can live a fulfilling life using their natural gifts and talents. Doing so will enable people to have a thriving body, soul, and spirit.

My ministry, like this book, is focused on tearing down spiritual, emotional, and physical strongholds so that all people can live free. I have helped develop a wholistic healing method called Inside Out that identifies and uproots the cause of unhealthy strongholds so that the individuals are empowered to break free and to live vibrant victorious lives. Key components of this healing process are included in this book. But for individual or group sessions to dive deeper in your healing journey you can request at www.sarahmacleod.org.

I am privileged to have co-led Harvest Sound International church with my husband, Scott, since 1993 in Nashville, Tennessee. Our Church is passionate about healing and equipping individuals to live out their God given potentials and to operate in their divine designs. In 2007, Scott and I founded a ministry school called Harvest Sound Intensive, which trains servant-hearted leaders to transform their specific spheres of influence. For more information on the church or ministry school go to: harvestsound.com.

When I'm not working, I love cycling to my favorite parks in my city, long walks in nature, playing corn hole with my family, sipping on chai tea, and eating healthy dishes from all over the world.

I invite you to connect with me at www.sarahmacleod.org or to visit me on Instagram @sarah_macleod7.

NOTES

1. *Cambridge Dictionary*, s.v. "stronghold" (n.), accessed 10/15/2022, https://dictionary.cambridge.org/us/dictionary/english/stronghold.

2. Strong's Concordance, *Bible Hub*, s.v. "ochuróma (n.)," accessed March 27, 2023, https://biblehub.com/greek/3794.htm.

3. Strong's Concordance, *Bible Hub*, s.v. "nekros (adj.)," accessed October 23, 2023, https://biblehub.com/greek/3498.htm.

4. "India Population (Live)," worldometer, accessed October 23, 2023, https://www.worldometers.info/world-population/india-population/.

NOTES

5. "Church Dropouts Have Risen to 64%—But What About Those Who Stay," Barna, accessed 10/24/2022, https://www.barna.com/research/resilient-disciples/.

6. Donald Miller, *A Million Miles in a Thousand Years: What I Learned While Editing My Life,* (Nashville, Thomas Nelson), accessed on Goodreads, https://www.goodreads.com/work/quotes/2003288-a-million-miles-in-a-thousand-years-what-i-learned-while-editing-my-lif

7. "Student Suicides Increase By 70% Between 2011 And 2021: NCRB Data," Outlook India, accessed October 23, 2023, https://www.outlookindia.com/national/student-suicides-increase-by-70-between-2011-and-2021-ncrb-data-news-317044.

8. Bill Johnson, *Quotefancy,* accessed March 24, 2023, https://quotefancy.com/quote/1516419/Bill-Johnson-Perfectionism-is-the-counterfeit-of-excellence-Excellence-is-Kingdom-while.

9. Eric Fromm, *QuotesLyfe,* accessed March 7, 2023, https://www.quoteslyfe.com/quote/Not-he-who-has-much-is-rich-564181.

10. Martin Luther King, Jr., *BrainyQuote,* accessed March 24, 2023, https://www.brainyquote.com/quotes/martin_luther_king_jr_297516

11. *Cambridge Dictionary,* s.v. "prejudice" (n.), accessed 10/24/2022,

https://dictionary.cambridge.org/us/dictionary/english/prejudice.

12. *Online Etymology Dictionary,* s.v. "prejudice" (v.), accessed 10/24/2022, https://www.etymonline.com/word/prejudice#etymonline_v_1 9410.

13. Hillary Mayell, "India's 'Untouchables' Face Violence, Discrimination," *National Geographic,* accessed March 27, 2023, https://www.nationalgeographic.com/pages/article/indias-untouchables-face-violence-discrimination.

www.ingramcontent.com/pod-product-compliance
Lightning Source LLC
Chambersburg PA
CBHW070858160726
48004CB00003B/1139